SHAKEN,
Not Stirred

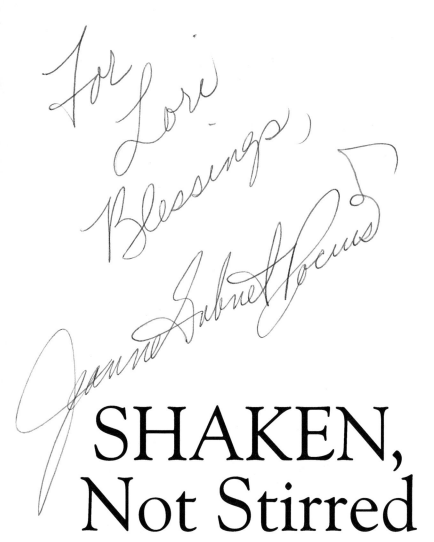

For Lori —
Blessings,
Jeanne Gabriel Pocius

SHAKEN,
Not Stirred

A SURVIVOR'S ACCOUNT OF THE
JANUARY 12, 2010 EARTHQUAKE IN HAITI

Jeanne G. Pocius

Outskirts Press, Inc.
Denver, Colorado

With love and appreciation I dedicate this book to the brave and resilient people of the nation of Haiti:

N'ap kapab ak l'aide du bondieu

Outskirts Press, Inc.
http://www.outskirtspress.com

ISBN: 978-1-4327-5835-6

Library of Congress Control Number: 2010934409

Outskirts Press and the "OP" logo are trademarks belonging to Outskirts Press, Inc.

PRINTED IN THE UNITED STATES OF AMERICA

Acknowledgements

First and foremost, my deepest thanks to all the staff and faculties of the Ecole de Musique Ste Trinite in Port-au-Prince and the annex in Petion Ville (Pere David Cesar, Mme Nicole St Victor, et al), and the Ecole de Musique Dessaix-Baptiste (Fritz Velascot, Fabrice LaFond, Alland Lamour, et al) in Jacmel, and all the other music schools with which I have been blessed to work, and to the priests and sisters of St Margaret and our beloved Evecque of the Episcopal Diocese of Haiti, Bishop Jean Zache Duracin, for continuing to support music and arts education and vocations in Haiti.

Special thanks to the the sainted Sister Anne Marie Bickerstaff, who watches over our work from Heaven, as do those sainted members of our community who were lost on January 12, 2010 and after, and my beloved Sourp Hayr Sourp Tsolag Oshagan Minassian, and grandmother Isabel Constance "Gram" Perkins.

Thanks, too, to all the many volunteers who have contributed instruments, time, money and effort to seeing music education continue and thrive in Haiti. Too numerous to list all by name, but especially John Jost of Bradley University and Janet Anthony of

Lawrence University, who first encouraged me to come to Haiti.

And thanks to all my colleagues in education in Haiti, especially my beloved brothers and sisters, including Pierre Leroy, Edgard "Gaguy" Depestre, Rene Jean-Jumeau, Vitalem Alriche (now in Canada) and all the junior professors at each school. I love you all madly!

In addition, many thanks to Nick Mondello for writing the introduction to this book, and to Professor Paul Morris, head of the graduate writing program at Arizona State University in Phoenix for his sage advice in the process and context of this work.

And thanks to Dr. Laennec Hurbon for his insights into Haitian history and culture, which have proven invaluable to me.

Many thanks to the journalists who continue to fight the good fight and have help to publicize our needs in Haiti, particularly Mandalit del Barco from NPR, and Ken Kidd from the Toronto Star. We need more journalists like them. In these days of designer-brand news, I have been honored to meet and know these true denizens of the search for Truth.

Thanks also to Madames Florence Elie and Gladys Lauture, who have provided hospitality to me, and to Drs Jean Philippe Harvel "Velo" Duverseau and Jean Serge Dorismond who provided me with medical evaluation and treatment for my quake injuries and illnesses.

Thanks to the staff of Outskirts Press for once again providing me with excellent service and advice in the publishing of this, my second work to be published by them.

Thanks to my partners at Instrumental Change, Inc: Martin Rooney, Esquire, Mark Schwartz, CPA, and Ms. Bonnie Lowell for their genius and loving encouragement every step of the way, and to those members of my church family at Holy Trinity Armenian Apostolic Church, in Cambridge, MA, especially Der Hayr Vasken Kouzouian and Direhayr Hayr Mampre Kouzouian, for your continuing prayerful support.

Many thanks to the international trumpet community, especially Michael Anderson of TPIN (Trumpet Players' International Network), and the ITG(International Trumpet Guild) who came to my aid in my hour of greatest need: we are a brotherhood of love and music that is eternal! Because of you people were housed, fed and educated at a time when all those things were in very short supply. God bless you all.

And the greatest thanks of all to my Lord and Savior and ever-living God, Jesus Christ, Who continues to strengthen and inspire me in my daily walk in His footsteps.

Blessings, Jeanne

Table of Contents

Foreword

One evening at New York's Blue Note during an extended break between hard-charging jazz tunes, the late legendary trumpeter, Maynard Ferguson, chatted with the audience. Ferguson, right off of a screaming high-note cadenza that seemed to peel paint, thanked the audience for their attendance and support and mentioned what an thrill it was to be there. He then paused for a second, extended his beautiful golden trumpet out over his outstretched arms and said, half-jokingly "what an honor it was to play God's instrument." The audience, consisting of fans and more than a few trumpet players (who immediately caught the unintended dual meaning of the comment) cackled a bit. The banter continued then Ferguson and the band moved on to the next screamer.

As I sat there and later on the way home, I thought more about Maynard's comment and began reflecting on my own trumpet-playing and music career. Yes, I said a "Thank you, God!" for being so very blessed to play trumpet. I also felt humbled and thankful for the friendships both business-wise and more personal with which I have been blessed through my 50-plus years in music.

I first met Jeanne Pocius some years back through the various "geek" websites and chat forums many of us trumpeters frequent. Jeanne seemed to be a very active, ongoing contributor. In reading her various comments, I surmised that here was a person, a top pro trumpeter known around the world, who - without reservation, remuneration and with apparent complete selflessness - was offering sage counsel to those trumpeters with damaged horns, embouchures and spirits. What really amazed me was not only the evident genius in her counsel, but, her complete and sincere willingness to help total strangers.

I eventually got to meet Jeanne in person and, by taking a number of lessons from her, a friendship grew. I later had the privilege of helping Jeanne a bit with her first highly-acclaimed book, "Trumpeting by Nature" (Outskirts Press). The more I learned about Jeanne, her own life's ups and downs, the more I became aware and in awe of a person of enormous talent and genius, kindness, faith and utter love for her fellow human beings. Jeanne is, as the sports analysts say (and to turn a phrase trumpetwise) "an impact player."

When she advised all of us acolytes in the trumpet "world" that she would soon leave the United States and become a "musical missionary" teaching the men and women musicians of Haiti, many wondered and silently questioned her sanity. Here was one of the world's foremost and well-known trumpeter/educators, an accomplished pro performer (she's performed with some of the finest show biz acts) and teacher/clinician, "packing her school teaching day gig in" (when she didn't have to, so that another teacher could keep her job) to answer a much higher calling. I guess making that decision and implementing it was something you might expect from a trumpet player whose middle name is "Gabriel" - a trumpeting angel!

"*Shaken, Not Stirred,*" of course is a wry quip taken from the James Bond books and, later, movies. Here 007-octave Jeanne tells both a heart-wrenching and heart-warming tale. Beware: it is not an easy read. When Jeanne describes the utter tragedy, desperation, frustration and calamitous aftermath that befell the people of Haiti in the January earthquake, one cannot help but be overwhelmed. Her no-holds-barred description of the wounded and the dead shook me. Her valiant attempts - that's my description, as I assure you Jeanne's humility will spring from these pages - and efforts to provide first aid for the wounded men, women and children is truly heroic. From the very first tremors, we're swept up in a tale of selflessness and will to help others survive — even as she herself was wounded, became ill and persevered on the fuel of Faith.

What is *not* detailed here in these pages is the frantic, panicked attempt of friends and musicians worldwide to secure knowledge of Jeanne's safety and whereabouts during this horrific crisis. *"She's dead!"* wrote one individual across the Internet. Another: *"No! Her school was destroyed but no one has heard from her or found her body!"* As I read these minute-by-minute "updates," I saw what a love and respect the trumpet world has for Jeanne Pocius. Along with friends and fellow trumpeters Mark Schwartz in Arizona, Terry Casey (who called me daily) and Barb Chickosky in Boston, Glenn Bengry in Detroit, Pat Shaner and Jerry Donato and many others, through Facebook and chatrooms we became personally enmeshed in this story. The fear, the love and concern that these men and women had for their "Chop Doc" was uncanny. However, it was no surprise. While "Everyone" might "Love Raymond" on TV, these and other trumpet folk absolutely adored their guru. The data bits of love and concern flew at light speed across the Internet. Still no word about Jeanne after a week. Then, a Facebook update by Glenn Bengry stated and then confirmed that Jeanne, who was completely incommunicado as you will see, had been sighted - wounded and worn, but, indeed alive.

Celebrities, notables and politicos all blazed across our television screens asking for us to help financially. It sure was easy for me to go to my PC and zap in $10 online to the Salvation Army and move on. Reading Jeanne's story, I wonder how I would have fared in this situation. I assure you I'm nowhere near as brave.

I'd guess it's a validation of Jeanne's love for the Haitian people that, when offered to be evacuated with other Americans, she declined and opted to remain in Haiti and serve her fellow Man. Very Jeanne-like.

When Jeanne Pocius arrived in Boston's Logan Airport on April 16, to her surprise an array of trumpeters drawn nationwide was present to perform a specially-composed "fanfare" for her arrival at the gate. It was a surprise "party." No movie star, politician or big-wig could have gathered so much talent and heart for that kind welcome. However, it probably pales by comparison to the welcome Jeanne Pocius will get when she returns to Haiti this year to continue her personal journey of teaching - about trumpet, love and Life.

Maynard Ferguson might have played "God's instrument" but, you will see that the true instrument of God here is one Jeanne Gabriel Pocius. So, Dear Reader I humbly offer you Jeanne Pocius' *Shaken Not Stirred*. Her story shakes and stirs my soul. It will yours, too.

Nick Mondello, New York, New York

The Day the World Changed Forever

It was just another ordinary day, a Tuesday, the 12th of January, 2010, in downtown Centreville (center of the city), Port-au-Prince, Haiti. I had returned to Port-au-Prince to continue my ministry of trumpet performance and education. We had big plans to build new schools and to develop programs for existing schools.

We had begun to rehearse for the second annual Fest du Trompette on January 31st, again to benefit the St. Croix (Holy Cross) hospital in Leogane. This year we would do the trumpet festival performance off-site, at the Karib Convention Center, in Petion Ville, in hopes of attracting a larger audience and garnering more support for our recently reopened hospital.

Businesses were open and schools were in session, with each school's children wearing color-coded uniforms denoting their school and grade level. For example, at Holy Trinite the little boys wore gray uniforms and the little girls wore green jumpers with white blouses. In middle school, the boys wore white shirts with green plaid trim and the girls wore green plaid skirts with white blouses.

Street vendors hawked their wares, shouting in sing-song or

nasal stridency, and competing for the loudest and most invasive advertisements of their wares.

Colorfully decorated *"Tap-Taps"* (public buses) transported their passengers through congested streets with much blaring of horns and bravado, causing a perpetual haze of pollution and dust and noise to hang over the city.

It was just another ordinary day, a Tuesday, in downtown Port-au-Prince.

I rose from my bed in the rose room of the guest house of the Holy Trinity complex and took a bucket shower in the bathroom since the cold tap water was not running today. I savored a cup of Marlene's strong black Haitian coffee (with far too many spoons full of sugar, as is the custom in Haiti) and enjoyed a sandwich made from "Mamba" peanut butter (with hot peppers) and grape-fruit jelly.

I spoke with Pere David Cesar, Canon of the Holy Trinity Cathedral and Director of the Music School, who asked me to enlarge a couple of scores which I had orchestrated for the upcoming Trumpet Festival.

Since we did not have facilities to enlarge scores with a copier at the school, I called my "adopted" big brother, Edgard "Gaguy" Depestre, to ask if there was anywhere in Port-au-Prince with the capacity to enlarge documents.

"As a matter of fact, there is" he said.

"And that would be…?"

"Bur-o-Matic" he crowed triumphantly.

"Okay, would it be possible to get it done today?"

"Sure, come on down."

So I found myself walking three blocks north of Ste. Trinite, down Rue Pavee, to Rue de Centre and the offices of Bur-o-Matic, the biggest office machine store in Haiti.

Gaguy, as Technical Director, was in charge of training new technicians in analyzing and repairing large office machines, mostly copiers.

We examined his car, which had been hit by an errant motorcyclist who was speeding through Jacmel the previous weekend, and was being repaired in the driveway next to the building.

Gaguy took the two scores to the copy center next door, and brought me up to his office to sit and chat while we waited for the copying to be finished.

He introduced me to his friend and boss, Lionel Volel, and to the technicians from his latest class who were busy with a machine in the next room, and periodically asking for advice from the "Majestreaux" (another of Gaguy's nicknames).

Gaguy also showed me a new shortcut to enhance my skills with the FINALE music writing program.

After about an hour and a half, Gaguy called to see if the copies were done and learned that the first score was done, but the second would take a bit longer, since a paying customer had arrived with an emergency project that bumped our charity project.

"*Pa gen problem*" I piped, in Kreyol.

"I can drop it off at Ste. Trinite on my way home" said Gaguy.

"Great. Thanks." I said as I left.

As I walked up the Rue Pavee, returning to the Holy Trinity Complex (which included an elementary school and a professional school, as well as the music school and the Cathedral), I noted the usual street kitchens serving up a savory choice of Haitian lunches cooked over charcoal or propane fires, including fried chicken and *cabrit* (goat), or fried hot dogs, rice and beans, and occasionally fried "*banann*"(plantains, soaked in lime juice, then deep-fried) served with a really spicy hot cole slaw called "*pickelese.*"

The delicious smells of cooking food competed with the smells of sweaty bodies and overindulgent colognes, dusty streets, exhaust from cars and *tap-taps,* and occasional heaps of garbage on the corners.

Dinner "*din-NAY*" is the main daily meal in Haiti, served in the afternoon.

Young boys walked by, hawking small plastic packets of water "*Dlo frais*" ("de-low fray" or "cold water"), which they carried in huge burlap bags balanced on a rolled towel atop their heads. Other vendors sold soda ("*gazeuse*") or household supplies, or pills (vitamins or Tylenol or herbs, mostly, in blister packs) of every size, shape and color.

I arrived back at Ste. Trinite a little after 2 pm. Cues of parents milled about outside the school courtyard, awaiting the dismissal of the elementary students, whose grey and white and green uniforms identified their school and grade level.

As I walked into the schoolyard, the elementary students were lining up for dismissal. Dozens of parents crowded the alleyway outside the gates. Junior high school students were jumping hurdles and doing gymnastics under the watchful eyes of their coach, having tryouts for a track team. I slapped high-fives with two of them: Jeannot, a first trumpet player in the EIV Concert Band and his friend, oboist Beauvais.

It was just an ordinary day, a Tuesday, at Ste. Trinite School, in Port-au-Prince.

I entered the passageway beneath the stairs which led to the gift/craft shop and the guest house and climbed the stairs to the guest house refectory.

I sat down to dinner with Pere David Cesar and some of the music school office staff. I inquired about his health (he had had "la grippe" the Haïtian term for a chest cold-flu bug) and we discussed the upcoming 50th anniversary concert of the Petit Chanteurs Men's and Boys' Choir, and the loan of a violin to a visiting American doctor who would be arriving the 16th and needed to practice while he was volunteering at a medical clinic.

We discussed emails from Janet Anthony, director of strings at Lawrence University in Wisconsin who served as co-director of the summer music camps in Leogane and Jacmel, and had been the person who had first invited me to come to Haiti. Then we discussed Jean-Gerald, our talented young oboist, who might be going to a double- reed conference in Brazil.

Marlene, the cuisinaire ("cook") had prepared a meal of a beef and vegetable ragout with white rice. (I remember that for some reason I drank a lot more water than usual).

As usual, "Mimi" the little housecat of the guest house was begging for food next to my chair, since she knew that I would give in and share a part of my meal with her.

As I was finishing dinner, I received a call from Madame Florence Elie, the Protectrix (ombudsman) of the Republic of Haiti, who is a dear friend. A generous donor in the US had donated a year's worth of rent on an efficiency apartment for me, since I was spending so much time in Haiti.

Florence had just the place: in Turgeau, above the house in which her mother had lived. She was sending a driver to pick me up and bring me to her office, from which we would drive to the apartment.

Dominic (or "Do-Do") arrived in an SUV to take me to the OPC (*Office de la Protection des Citoyens et Citoyennes*).

This was a large, former home, which housed several offices now. I met all of Florence's staff, and then I had a brief tour of the facilities. Florence was particularly proud to introduce me to "Pappy Marc" Lamarre, director of the *Jazz des Jeunes* musical ensemble.

We left the OPC and ascended up into Turgeau, through Canape Vert, busy as always with throngs of students, business people, the street-side marketplace, and artists selling paintings in the bright Haitian "primitive" style, to Turgeau 29.

The apartment was situated high on a hill with a beautiful view of downtown Port-au-Prince and the harbor. I remember taking a photograph with my Kodak/Motorola Zn5 Motozine cameraphone of the Notre Dame Catholic Cathedral (which was near Ste. Trinite) from the end of the driveway.

The pinks and whites of the cathedral contrasted with the bright turquoise and deeper blue of the water in the harbor, and the brilliant greens of foliage throughout the city. Here, away from the cacophony of traffic in the center of the city, I could appreciate the beauty of downtown Port-au-Prince in a new way. I expected that this view would become a favorite of mine as I commuted daily from the apartment in the future.

We went inside and viewed the main room, kitchenette and bathroom of the small but neatly organized apartment. We discussed the cost of purchasing an *inverter* (an electronic device for converting battery power from car batteries into power for the electrical outlets) or a gasoline-powered generator for the apartment, and that this would be wiser than relying upon EDH (Electrical Department de Haiti, the national electrical company). We also discussed how to get a refill of the propane tank for the gas stove, and replacing the twin-sized bed with a full or queen-sized bed.

I handed Florence the deposit and she handed me the keys to the apartment.

As we were leaving, I was delighted to meet her daughter, Guisella "Guisou", who lived in the larger apartment downstairs (the house and apartments were built into the side of the hill, with the efficiency apartment on the top floor).

We returned down the mountain to "La Ville" and Ste Trinite. It was about 3:15 pm and I received a call from Gaguy, saying that the scores were all done and he would bring them to me on his way home. I told him I was on my way back and would definitely be there about 4:30 or so since I had jazz ensemble rehearsal at 5 pm.

He explained that he had to get home and would drop off the scores in the morning on his way to work. We joked about sharing morning coffee and he said "Okay, let me go so I can beat the traffic!" (This is always an issue in the late afternoon in Port-au-Prince). I said "Love you so much, *au demain* ("until tomorrow)" and we hung up.

Then I received a text from my friend, clarinetist Michee Charlot, who served on the National Police Force, and played in the Palace Band, telling me he had to work late and could not attend jazz band today. I called him to ask if he was also cancelling his lesson with my friend, Laënnec Hurbon, at 4 pm.

"Have you spoken with Laënnec?" he asked.

"No, what's up?"

"I texted him, but have not heard back from him. I do have to cancel his saxophone lesson today because I have to work late."

"No problem, I will call him" I said, and promptly did so. This was about 3:40 pm.

"Laënnec, Michee asked me to call you and tell you that he has to cancel your lesson because he has to work late"

"Yes, I received the message" he said. "I am coming down to jazz band rehearsal. I will be on-time" (referring to a recent conversation about confusion with starting times for rehearsals and the all-too-prevalent tardiness habit in Haiti).

In Haiti, as in much of the Caribbean, there is a societal disregard for the clock. Thus an appointment or meeting which was scheduled for 4 pm might not occur until 5 pm or 7 pm, or not until the next day. I remember one time on another Caribbean island when I asked about the time of a scheduled flight and was told that it might leave at 11 am, or 12 pm, or maybe at 9 am. As a result, I learned to take time as "relative".

"Are you sure? You don't have to come just for jazz band" I said.

"*Absolumente, m'ap vini* (Absolutely, I'm coming). I am looking forward to it. I will be on-time" he repeated.

"*D'accord* (okay)" I said and hung up.

I greeted Jean Bernard Desinat, the conductor of the Petit Chanteurs Men's and Boys' choir at Ste. Trinite. With him was Ruth, the girlfriend of my adopted son, trumpeter Carlot Dorve, and Louis Jean-Renèl, the best counter tenor in the PC.

It was just another day, a Tuesday, an ordinary day in the Ste. Trinite School in Port-au-Prince.

I went through the alley to the Guest House and climbed the stairs to get my briefcase with the hand-outs I would use with Jazz Band in our 5 pm rehearsal.

I remember changing into flip-flops, but kept on my socks to protect against the ever-present, ravenous mosquitoes!

I put a bottle of water into my laptop bag with the music I'd printed off in the morning.

I was excited to introduce the jazz ensemble students to some new concepts in the blues book of Willie Thomas, donated by Jerry Donato, whom I'd recently met in Phoenix, Arizona.

Because I usually played piano in jazz band rehearsals, since we had had a hard time finding a reliable pianist, I left my Flip Oakes "Celebration" trumpet sitting on its trumpet stand on the floor in my room in the guest house. I also took the laptop out of the briefcase, and placed it, in its protective padded inner case on the extra bed in the room.

I grabbed a hand towel, since I expected it to be quite warm in the auditorium without the air conditioning, which was usually only turned on for concerts, and I knew I would "*bay dlo*"(literally "make water," in other words, sweat a lot!)

It was just an ordinary Tuesday afternoon at the Holy Trinity Music School.

I climbed down the stairs, bidding "*Bonne nuit*" (good night) to Marlene, our cook, who told me she had put something in the refrigerator for my supper before she left.

I also passed "Manmi Rose" the matriarch of the school, and Nicole St. Victor, the brilliant soprano and voice teacher at the school as they left for the day.

I then climbed the stairs from the courtyard up into the second floor of the elementary school which led to the entrance to the music school.

As I entered the downstairs rehearsal hall, on a level with the second floor of the elementary school and on the same level with the second floor of the professional school, I greeted the elderly gentleman who sat sentry at the gate to the stairs leading up to the music school proper.

Rumor had it that he had formerly been a member of the vicious "*ton-ton macoute*" vigilante police force which had terrorized ordinary citizens during the dictatorial reign of the Duvaliers. As usual, he was now docilely practicing hymns on his portable electronic keyboard.

At the top of the stairs, just outside Manmi Rose's office, I greeted Madame Ismique Lahens, the attendance officer for the music school, neatly attired in her starched grey uniform. She faithfully collected membership cards and noted attendance every day at the music school.

I received kisses on the cheeks from a few of the orchestra members who were in the hallway, and made my way down the stage right corridor into the *Salle Ste. Cecile* (St. Cecile Hall, the only full-sized concert hall in the country), passing the little open-air ante-chamber where some of the staff would eat their lunch and some students did their homework while waiting for their lessons.

As I entered the Ste. Cecile hall, I saw and heard my godson, Jean Remy, who was practicing the string bass center stage in preparation for his bass lesson with Ariane Saul, the principal bassist of the OPST (Orchestre Philharmonique du Sainte Trinite, the school's symphony orchestra). I noted his good, strong tone and steady bow arm appreciatively.

A few of my jazz ensemble students had arrived already (it was then about 4:40 pm).

At 4:45, Remy moved into the studio 24 hallway (stage left of the auditorium) to have his lesson, and we moved onto the stage.

I went to the piano, which was up stage left, with the keys facing the back wall, just downstage of the upstage left entry onto the stage.

I placed my laptop bag on a chair next to the piano, placed my water bottle on the piano and my calendar book and phone on the desk of the piano.

Trumpeter David Saintilus, the youngest member of the jazz ensemble, assisted me in setting up three rows of chairs facing the piano. We would be working on jazz improvisation today.

I called the other trumpet players: Guemali Dorneval, Rock Olson, Fleury and Pipot St. Surin up onto stage briefly to change a trumpet ensemble rehearsal from Wednesday afternoon to Thursday afternoon, due to a work conflict for one of the other trumpeters.

Three saxophonists had also arrived: Canes and Charles Charlemagne (both of whom played alto, as did Laënnec Hurbon, who had not yet arrived), and Dominique Lexide (who played tenor sax).

A few students were expected to be late: trombonists Leone and Jameson, drummer Jeobaham, and trumpeter Pierre Richard Etienne, all of whom were coming from jobs.

The trumpeters went back to their cases, and I played a few riffs on the piano to warm-up, and then stood up to pass out papers on the chairs we had set up.

It was just an ordinary day, a Tuesday, in the Holy Trinity Music School of Port-au-Prince, Haiti.

The Beginnings of Change

In January of 2004, I fell and broke my right leg in an accident at the Cove School, in Beverly, Massachusetts, which was one of the six elementary schools in which I ran beginning band programs for the public school system. This led to an extended period of time on crutches and in a wheelchair. That time taught me to be far more aware of the inaccessibility of most of the world to persons with physical disabilities.

The break was of a crumbling nature on the tibial plateau (bulging section of the tibia bone), which meant that it would lead eventually (inevitably) to a total knee replacement. (For me, this would occur in March of 2007. Months of rehabilitation and physical therapy followed).

The advantage to all of this was more time to reflect, pray and read and study.

During this time period, a powerful movie was released: Mel Gibson's "Passion of the Christ" was a painful movie to view. I sat in a darkened theater, in my wheelchair, and wept at the depiction of our Lord's passion, torture and crucifixion.

My best friend through all of this was my priest and mentor, *Hayr*

Sourp ("Holy Father", like a Monsignor in the Catholic Church, a high priest of the Armenian Apostolic Church) Tsolag "Oshagan" Minassian. *Hayr Sourp* was an incredibly learned man, who had earned doctoral degrees in both Theology and Music, founded an orchestra and chorale, and written several books- all after he had broken his neck in a swimming accident fifty years earlier.

I first met Father Minassian when his former first trumpet player in the Erevan Orchestra of Cambridge, Massachusetts was unable to play for a concert. His substitute became ill on the day before the concert, and the concertmaster, Michael Loo, contacted me late on Saturday evening to play for the Sunday evening performance.

I arrived an hour early for the concert, and went through all of the music with Father, then sight-read the performance. Because I performed well, I was invited to become the new principal trumpeter for the orchestra.

I continued to play with the orchestra for many years, and grew in friendship with Hayr Sourp. We would speak, sometimes for several hours at a time, on a regular weekly basis.

Perhaps one of his greatest gifts was his prodigious memory: Hayr Oshagan had memorized many thousands of jokes, all clean, and all funny, as well as countless inspirational stories. He had organized them in his mind so that if you mentioned any subject to him, he would be able to tell you 4 or 5 jokes concerning that subject.

When Hayr Sourp's mother, who had cared for him ever since his accident nearly fifty years earlier, passed away in early 2004, I began to call him several times each day. I thought that if I asked him to tell me a joke, he would laugh in the process, and I knew that laughter would be healing for him.

Our discussions were broad-ranging, covering theology, the nature of handicap-access, literature, music, history, politics, almost any subject you could imagine.

Through Hayr Sourp's influence I began to study the Armenian language, with its different forms and dialects (Western Modern, Classical, and Eastern) and became a member of the Holy Trinity Armenian Apostolic Church, for which he served as choir director. I began a spiritual odyssey of development and discovery that continues to this day.

One Sunday morning, while kneeling in the choir (below the altar of the church, which is Orthodox in nature so the altar is raised above the congregation and choir, and sometimes concealed behind a curtain), I experienced a powerful vision.

The main doors at the back of the church, facing toward the altar, opened and a brilliant, white light streamed into the church.

Gradually a tall, thin figure was revealed, robed and sandaled and carrying a shepherd's crook.

As this figure walked down the central aisle of the church, He would tap a person on the shoulder and that person would rise and follow Him down the aisle.

When the Man reached me, He tapped me on the shoulder and said "Jeanne, I call you."

I rose and followed Him, knowing that no matter where He led me, I would willingly and eagerly go.

Little did I know at the time just where that calling would take me.

A Summer of Loss

In May of 2007, my beloved Grandmother, Isabel Constance Perkins, who had lived with me for some time, was diagnosed with a relapse of breast cancer. Gram had been through a mastectomy five years earlier, at the age of 93, and at the time had refused any chemotherapy, believing that the slow-growing nature of her tumor would prevent a recurrence during the rest of her life.

Sadly, this was not the case. Once the cancer reappeared, it attacked her with a vengeance that would not be denied, including a very painful eruption of "fungation". This is a manifestation of breast cancer in which the skin thickens and toughens. A crusty layer resembling alligator skin develops and the skin cracks open, revealing the inner layers of tissue.

She begged me to keep her in our East Boston apartment, (not to send her to a hospital or nursing- home) and thanks to Beacon Hospice, I was able to do so.

We moved a hospital bed into the living room, and began the slow dance of saying goodbye.

Gram was a beautiful woman, who had always been very elegant: perfectly coiffed hair, beautiful accessories, stylishly dressed.

She was always a bit of a coquette and would flirt with gentlemen visitors up until the day before her passing on July 26th, 2007.

At the same time, she was a woman of faith: reading the Bible daily, reading inspirational magazines, singing hymns, praying.

She crocheted countless "lap-robes" (lap-sized blankets with a small pocket added for keys or other personal belongings) for elderly in nursing homes, hats and mittens for orphans in Armenia, afghans for family members' beds, etc.

In fact, when she was in her final coma, her hands were moving under the covers. When we lifted the covers, thinking she might be distressed, we discovered that her hands were continuing to crochet, even without the needles and yarn.

Two days before she passed away, after our Hospice workers, Nicole St. Laurent and Choupette Polisme (both from Haiti) left, Gram and I sat talking in the living room. By this time she was confined to her bed, as the cancer had spread to the bones of her left leg, leaving her unable to walk.

Gram, who was profoundly deaf now and only conversed by reading lips, looked at me and said

"I hear men's voices."

"Really, Gram?" I said, thinking that she had been hearing people talking in the other room for about a week, since she had been taking morphine. "What are they saying?"

She shook her head

"They're singing."

"Really? What are they singing, 'Amazing Grace'?" which was her favorite hymn.

She shook her head again, and tilted her head for several minutes, as though to listen more carefully.

She opened her eyes and looked deeply into my eyes. Her eyes were filled with a beautiful light:

"Glory to God in the Highest" she exclaimed triumphantly.

"Oh, Gram, you're hearing the angels in heaven!"

She nodded and closed her eyes to listen again, and drifted off to sleep.

Later that same evening, Gram experienced an episode of "terminal agitation." This is an episode of extreme mental and physical agitation, caused (I was told by the Hospice workers) by the brain stem's fighting against death, even as the body succumbs to it.

A nurse had come to check on Gram, because we had noticed that her breathing had become labored. The nurse, thinking that Gram was comatose, inserted a thermometer into her ear, startling Gram and setting off several hours of extreme shouting, and physical disturbances.

I knelt by Gram's bedside, stroking her arm, calling her by name "Gram, Gram, it's Jeannie, come back to me. Please, Gram."

I called my first cousin, Denise Lyon Anding, in Louisiana, who rose from bed with her husband, David, to join me in prayer.

Finally, after several hours on my knees, I attempted to rise, which caused me severe pain. I cried out in agony.

Gram came back to her senses immediately: her baby (old as I was) was in need. She had to respond.

She smiled at me, and asked "ice cream?" (Always her favorite snack).

I hobbled to the kitchen and got her a cup of ice cream, into which we mixed the medicine.

She ate half the cup, and then drifted into a peaceful sleep, which continued throughout much of the next day.

Thursday evening, after receiving extreme unction from our Pastor, Father Vasken Kouzouian, she passed from this life at 8:15 pm, July 26, 2007.

We waited several hours for a special nurse to come and declare her death, then for the undertakers.

It was after two a.m. when I fell into bed, exhausted, physically, mentally and emotionally.

As I drifted into sleep, I once again felt my Gram's arms surrounding me (as they had not been able to do since I was tiny, because she was so petite and I had grown large), as if to say "I'm okay now, thanks for everything."

A deep feeling of peace filled me and I slept.

The Call to Ministry

After Gram passed, I began to feel a strong impulse to pursue some sort of ministerial service.

I explored possibilities in several different areas: the Carmelite order of sisters, the Dominican order of sisters (Order of Preachers, O.P.), service as an Episcopal priest, or as an American Baptist or Congregational minister, or becoming involved in lay ministry.

I worked with several different vocational counselors, most notably Sister Cathy Arnold, of the Dominican Sisters of St. Mary of the Springs, and, of course, my beloved Armenian priests, Hayr Oshagan Minassian and my pastor, Father Vasken Kouzouian.

God was definitely calling me, but to where? To what type of service?

In the Fall of 2007 I returned to full-time work as elementary band director for the public schools of the City of Beverly, Massachusetts.

My schedule was whirl-wind: six different elementary schools, with a band rehearsal and group lessons for each. I taught lessons in all the different band instruments (flute, clarinet, saxophone, horn, trumpet, trombone, baritone horn, tuba, electric bass and percussion), including adaptive lessons for challenged students.

In the Fall, I had the busy task of collecting classroom schedules from each of 27 fifth-grade classrooms, then matching the different student instrument choices with those schedules to try and find lesson slots that would work for everyone, with the least amount of interruption of classroom schedules, given the drive to pass the infamous standardized state tests required each year.

This was complicated, too, by the need to accommodate the special needs students' therapy sessions, but I was determined that these children be involved, even more so since my own experiences of the past couple of years in dealing with a physical disability (and my continuing physical therapy after my knee surgery).

In the spring, word spread throughout the school system that massive budget cuts were forthcoming.

I knew that my program would be threatened, as the fine arts are always the first to suffer cuts in lean times.

What I did not know was how this would profoundly change my life.

Simple Email Request

Subject: [TPIN] volunteer in Haiti this summer opportunity
To: TPIN@tpin.okcu.edu

Guys and gals,

A colleague of mine has been teaching every summer in Haiti and tells me they are in desperate need of a brass instructor this summer due to a late cancellation. I don't have that many details but:

Trumpet teacher needed for music camp in Haiti - July 12-August 4

Teaching trumpet/directing band if able/jazz/coaching chamber groups

Most necessary qualifications: flexibility, good health and a good sense of humor

If interested, please contact ASAP Janet Anthony

By this time, I had learned that my program had, indeed, been cut from the school budget, and though I had been offered the opportunity to "bump" a less-senior teacher from her classroom music teaching position, I felt reluctant to do so because I was close to retirement age and had no family to support.

The younger teacher who would be affected had several young children, including one with a disability. To lose her job would cause a loss of medical benefits which would threaten her child's health. Thus I felt the only ethical option was to resign from my position with the public school system and I made the decision to enter some sort of religious life, be it a seminary program or a religious order.

I sent away for the information about the summer music camp, thinking I would send one of my adult trumpet students to gain further experience in teaching.

Then the bells began to chime: The school that ran the summer camp was the "Holy Trinity Music School" (my home church, of course, is the Holy Trinity Armenian Apostolic Church); the camp had been staffed in the past by members of the Boston Symphony Orchestra (including virtuoso trumpeter Roger Voisin, who had been a friend and a mentor to me, and the primary teacher of my first trumpeter/teacher, Bob Lemons); the camp was a church-sponsored activity, and provided only room and board as compensation, so it met the criteria for service as a missionary, which all of my vocational counselors felt was important prior to entering either an order or a seminary, and, of course, I would be teaching music (my passion).

I conferred with my priests, my vocational director, Sister Cathy Arnold, and family and friends; and I prayed for guidance.

Then I made the commitment, visited the Massachusetts General Hospital Travel Clinic to get my shots and prescriptions for Chloroquine (an anti-malarial medicine), and made the flight arrangements.

A Final Farewell

On the Sunday before I was to leave for Haiti, after *Badarak* (Armenian Apostolic Divine Liturgy) and before I left to go see Hayr Sourp Minassian at the hospital, Der Hayr Mampre Kouzouian, the retired pastor of our church and father of our pastor, blessed and anointed me for my mission in the Baptistery of the church.

> "God the Father, the Son and the Holy Spirit bless
> and protect you from all evil and enemies, internal
> and external, and bring you back safely to us. In the
> name of the Father and the Son and the Holy Spirit,
> now and always, unto the ages of ages. Amen."

Throughout all of my discernment process, my beloved friend, Hayr Sourp Oshagan Minassian had been my guide, my chief cheerleader, my confident, and my solace.

Sadly, earlier in the summer he had suffered a stroke, and was hospitalized. As a quadriplegic, his body chemistry could easily be upset: insufficient water or nutrients could cause major problems for him.

I visited him several times in the hospital that July before I left for Haiti and offered to postpone my trip until he was better enough to go home.

"Absolutely not" He thundered. "This is God's Will for you and you must go."

One did not argue with Hayr Sourp: ever!

But he was growing visibly weaker by the day, and I was concerned that I might lose him while I was gone.

"May I pray with you?" I asked him.

"By all means."

"Anoun Hor yev Vortvo yev Hokeet Sourbo" I began (In the name of the Father and the Son and the Holy Spirit, making the sign of the Cross).

Tears began to stream down my cheeks…

"Hayr Mer vor hergins yes; (Our father who art in heaven)
Soorb yeghitzi anoon ko. (Hallowed be thy name.)
Yegetze arkayootyoon ko; (Thy kingdom come)
Yeghitzin gamk ko vorbes (Thy will be done)
Hergins yev hergri. (On earth as it is in heaven)
Uzhatz mer hanabazort door mez aysor. (Give us this day our daily bread.)
Yev togh mez uzbardis mer, (And forgive us our trespasses)
Vorbes yev menk toghoomk merotz bardabanantz. (As we forgive those who trespass against us)
Yev mi danir uzmez ee portzootyoon; (And lead us not into temptation)
Ayl purgya uzmez ee chareh. (But deliver us from evil)
Ziko e arkayootyoon yev zorootyoon yev park havidyans, Amen.
(For the kingdom, the power and the glory are yours, now and forever, Amen.)"

"Bravo" he said, smiling at his pupil.

I kissed his cheek.

"I will see you tomorrow?" I asked, fully expecting that God would call him home that very Sunday evening.

"Okay, then."

But God did not take him home that night, and I was able to visit and pray with and for him for the next three days, until I had to leave for Haiti on Thursday.

On the day I left, I placed my hand on Hayr Sourp's chest.

"I'm taking your heart with me."

I brought my hand to my own chest, then back to his.

"And I'm placing my heart in your chest."

I gently kissed my fingertips and touched them to his lips and then to my own. I made the American Sign Language sign for "I love you" and turned to walk from the hospital room. . .

Suddenly "God be with you" Hayr Sourp roared in full voice, which I had not heard from him for many, many months.

I nodded. "See you soon" I called, smiled, waved, and walked away quickly to hide my tears.

First Summer in Haiti

When I first stepped off the airplane into the heat of a Haitian July, I felt pretty excited about the new adventures to come. I had no idea that my life had changed, and that I would spend the rest of my life working to improve the lives of my Haitian students and friends and those who would come to be my "family members" in Haiti and beyond.

I entered the terminal to the sounds of a Kompa band playing traditional Haitian music, with its syncopated beat patterns, simple and sweet melodies and lilting Kreyol lyrics.

Then came the long lines at Immigration, where my passport was stamped with a visa and I received a green card that I was to carry on my person as long as I stayed in Haiti and return when I left in August.

My bags were taken care of by one of the Holy Trinity Music School staff who came to the airport, collected my baggage tags and led me to a diplomatic lounge (air-conditioned) to wait as he collected the checked luggage.

We got into a large, white truck/van, and made the trip into town. Our first stop was at the Holy Trinity Music School itself.

Along the way from the airport, I was impressed by the colors of buildings and clothing and by the myriad activities: street vendors, motorcycles, brightly decorated trucks (I later learned were called *"tap-taps"* for the tapping the passengers made when they had reached their stops and called *"merci"* ("thank-you") to the driver).

There were many children, hopping onto the backs of trucks as they drove past, begging at every corner: *"grand gou* ("I'm so hungry"…one dollah." They would shout as they rushed the vehicle carrying a *blanc* (white person).

Finally we arrived at the Holy Trinity School complex, which looked a lot like parochial schools back in the States. My driver (whom I later learned was "Paul") led me upstairs to meet Nicole Ste. Victor in the music school.

I slipped on the staircase leading up to the second floor of the elementary school and fell, bruising my knees. Paul rushed back to help me, rubbing at the bruises to lessen the pain.

Soon I was ushered into Nicole's office on the third floor of the building. She was most gracious, asking about my background, welcoming me, and best of all, she spoke fluent English!

She told me that the camp was about a half hour away, but that we must stop enroute to pick up bottles of treated (clean) water.

So back down the stairs we went, back into the truck, and began the trip out of town.

Trip to Leogane

This trip was not as entertaining as the ride from the airport.

We drove through a poorer section of town, where automobile and motorcycle repairs were done on the sidewalks. Street vendors here were fewer, and more poorly clothed. Children and animals were far less healthy, with rags for clothing and bones visible through their skin.

I began to be worried---very worried about my decision to come to Haiti.

I saw pigs wallowing in streams of water on the side of the road...then realized that children were playing and people were bathing, washing clothes and collecting drinking water downstream from the pigs.

We passed huge garbage heaps where filthy, nearly naked children with the red hair, stick-thin arms and legs and swollen bellies of proteinuria (a disease of starvation), competed with wild dogs and goats and huge pigs for measly scraps.

The children squatted amid the trash and consumed whatever they found that might resemble food.

I began to weep, and had to close my eyes to keep from seeing more pain.

How could a music camp make a difference for such as these?

I felt totally inadequate and thought I should ask to be taken back to the airport to take the next flight home.

Then we arrived at the camp and I met "my kids" and began to teach my trumpeters immediately.

Here was my beloved son-to-be, Carlot Dorve, and elegant, brilliant and charming Pierre Richard Etienne, and the sad poet-philosopher Garry Yonel Francoise. Little Ti-Jean and Mairdjelisa, Martine and Taina, Marc-Philippe and Philippe, Fleury, the good-humored young student-teacher, and David Saintilus, Guemali Dorneval, and more...

I fell in love with the kids, and with Haiti, and knew I would continue to stay and return again and again.

Meanwhile, I stayed in close touch with my pastor about Hayr Sourp's condition. I learned that he had begun to take painkillers the day after I left, but that he was resting well. I began to hope that he might recover.

First Trip to Jacmel

The band director at St. Trinite, and at the camp, was Pierre "Pierrot" Leroy. Pierre also taught at the Dessaix Baptiste Music School in Jacmel, his home town, and traveled there every Friday night for Jazz Band rehearsal, then returned to Leogane for the weekend rehearsals and performances at camp.

That first Friday, Pierre had a concert with the jazz ensemble. I asked if I could accompany him and perhaps "sit-in" (play along with) the jazz band.

"That would be great" he replied. And thus began my first contact with Jacmel.

The ride to Jacmel was terrifying: sharp turns and switchbacks through the mountains were abundant (and Pierre drove at alarming speeds, obviously well-acquainted with the roads). I found myself alternately gasping and holding my breath as we careened around the mountains at break-neck speed, with horn blaring at each corner.

But the views of the mountains, the sky, and eventually the bay of Jacmel were absolutely astounding. I grew more deeply in love with this country.

The jazz ensemble was composed of 16 musicians of varying abilities. We played some swing, some ballads, and some Latin pieces to a very appreciative crowd.

I was amused to see the reactions of the band members to a female "lead" trumpet player who could play lots of high notes powerfully. Pierre called upon me to play an improvised latin-style solo on "Oye, Como Va?" and the crowd and the band roared their approval as I soared higher and higher into the altissimo registers of the trumpet.

After the concert, I met several members of Pierre's family: Alix (a wonderful philosopher-poet-civic leader, who had been mayor of Jacmel), Franck (who was visiting from NY), Frito (a really fine electric bass player) and several nieces.

And then I met Edgard "Gaguy" Depestre, an amazing tenor saxophonist and flautist, who had been a founding member of the "Caribbean Sextet" a group involved early on in the Afro-Cuban jazz scene. Gaguy played his tenor for me as we sat enjoying ice-cold Haitian "Prestige" beer on the front porch of the Leroy family home across the street from the school.

He had a strong, meaty but mellow sound and a great style as he played several excerpts for me from the music of Antonio Carlos Jobim.

Gaguy would become an important part of my education about Haitian culture and language, and I now consider him to be my "big brother" in every way.

I slept in Pierre's brother's bed (Frito stayed with Pierre), and we left very early Saturday morning to return to Leogane.

Schedule in Leogane

We started every morning at the camp with a trumpet warm-up session I had designed, with pedal tones, lip slurs and crisp articulations resounding throughout the camp so that everyone memorized the sequence and it became a running joke at the end-of-camp banquet.

This was followed by a morning prayer service, then breakfast in the refectory.

Then "*repetitions*" (rehearsals), lessons, large and small ensembles and theory classes filled the day, punctuated by sharp blasts on a referee's whistle to mark changes of classes (I grew to hate the sound of that whistle, probably about as much as non-trumpeters grew to hate the trumpet warm-ups).

Dinner (lunch) was sometime between 1 pm and 3 pm, and afternoon rehearsals were followed by a "*Vespres*" evening prayer service before supper and the evening large ensemble rehearsals of Petit Chanteurs, Chamber orchestra and OPST (Orchestre Philharmonique de Ste. Trinite, the signature ensemble of the school).

Sometimes there were additional rehearsals after the OPST,

but in this first week I was usually too tired from the all day heat(14 hours) and would collapse into bed, pull the sheet over my head to escape the mosquitoes and fall fast asleep.

Church services at the Holy Cross Episcopal Church were early Sunday morning and were often packed, as well as very hot and very long.

But I learned that Pere (Father) David Cesar, the director of the OPST, was a very good preacher: animated, clear, scripturally based, and spirit-filled. I always enjoyed his sermons.

David was also a great solace to me in the weeks to come.

On Friday, the 23rd of July, I received word that my beloved friend, Hayr Sourp Oshagan Minassian, had slipped into a coma from which he was not expected to recover.

I was very concerned about this and ran up a very high cell-phone bill calling back and forth to Boston to check in with Father Vasken Kouzouian and family members.

On Sunday morning, July 27th, I awoke to a great feeling of peace. Somehow I knew what the message would be when I called Father Vasken.

"Der Hayr" I began. "What is the news about Hayr Sourp?"

"Hayr Sourp passed away about 8:30 pm last night."

"I had a feeling that was so when I awoke this morning."

We noted that Hayr Sourp had passed away almost to the minute one year after my beloved Gram and wondered if they were chatting in heaven at that very moment.

When I hung up, I called Hayr Sourp's sister, Alyce.

"Alyce, I'm so sorry"

She was unable to speak much, but told me that Hayr Sourp had told her he didn't want me to see him with his "eyes closed."

I repeated to her the ceremony of heart exchange I had made with Hayr Sourp before I left.

"So it wasn't his heart that stopped last night, but mine." I told her. "And any time you want to hear his heart beat, you come to me for a hug and you can hear his heart beating in my chest."

We both cried. I promised I would stay in touch about the funeral, which I did, helping to notify choir members and friends of

Hayr Sourp about the funeral.

That evening at the prayer service, I played and recited the "Hayr Mer" for the campers and told them about Hayr Sourp.

The love, hugs, and messages of condolence I received from all the campers and staff helped tremendously, but I knew that I would always believe Hayr Sourp was alive, since I had left him that way.

Pere David was especially kind and supportive to me through the grieving process, and I will always be grateful to him for this.

In the final concert of the camp, I played the "Prayer of St. Gregory" by Alan Hovhaness (an Armenian composer) in honor and memory of Hayr Sourp. We repeated the performance on the anniversary of his death on July 26, 2009, and I hope this will become an annual tradition.

Following the end of camp on July 27th, (with a wonderful banquet the night after the concert) I joined many of the staff and headed to Jacmel for three more weeks of camp in the seashore town.

Camp in Jacmel

The camp in Jacmel spread out across the downtown area. Some rehearsals, lessons and the concert took place in the main school building, some in an old building down the street, and others in a national school building several blocks away.

I was housed in the "Cuban" house, down the hill from the national school. My roommates were Elise, a flute-playing student from Lawrence University, and Rebecca, a percussionist who was doing post-doctoral studies in Haitian ethnic music.

I taught a brass warm-up class and trumpet lessons, worked with the band and jazz band, and played with the orchestra and the jazz band. I began to learn Kreyol, a Haitian dialect that mixed elements of French, English, Spanish, native Indian and African languages, with a puzzling grammar that bore no relationship to the Romance languages which I had studied all my life.

I also began to discuss philosophy with Pierre's brother, Alix. Alix is a devotee of Omraam Mikhail Aiivanhov, a Bulgarian philosopher who uses the energy, heat and light of the sun as a metaphor for God's presence and influence on us on a daily basis.

Alix gave me my first book of the Omraam's teaching (I now

own several), and I slowly made my way through the French text, and with the help of translators had some interesting and enlightening discussions with Alix.

I also had some lengthy discussions with Fritz Valescot, the director of the Dessaix-Baptiste Music School which sponsored the camp, about plans to build a new school to replace the current one in Jacmel, which was insufficient to the needs of the community.

An idea began to germinate, and after much prayer and reflection, I made a covenant with God and with Fritz that I would work to see this new school become a reality.

This also led to the development of ideas about building an extended conservatory program as an outgrowth of the Holy Trinity Music school program in Port-au-Prince, and eventually to the organization and development of my non-profit charitable corporation, _Instrumental Change, Inc_ (ICI).

The second week of the camp, we experienced a strong "tempest" with high winds and heavy rains. For the first time I experienced the Haitians' fear of rain.

Heavy rains often lead to landslides, increases in insect populations and disease. Because most Haitians do not have extra clothing or rain gear, many have a profound dislike of going out in the rain. I used to laugh at this, but after my longer-term experience in Haiti, I have come to respect this healthy caution myself.

This, as it turned out, would be the first of four hurricanes to hit Haiti between August and October in the summer and autumn of 2008.

The last week in Jacmel, I became very ill, with a high temperature, vomiting and diarrhea, weakness and severe muscle cramps, and severe headaches. Janet Anthony, the director of the Jacmel camp and the cello/strings director at Lawrence University, and my roommate at the Leogane camp, had Gaguy Depestre bring me from the Cuban house up to the rooming house next door to the Leroy family home so that she could watch over me better.

I had been taking the Chloroquine on a weekly basis, but perhaps had not started it long enough before coming to Haiti. The Anopheles mosquitoes, which were prevalent in Jacmel, carried the malaria spirochetes. It seemed I had contracted a case, even though I had taken the prophylactics (perhaps because I had gone to Jacmel so soon after arriving in Haiti).

Tests when I returned to the US confirmed this, and I began a program of medication to eradicate the spirochetes.

By Friday of that last week, I had recovered sufficiently to be able to rehearse and play some trumpet, so I did play for the Saturday night concert, dedicating the "Adagio" movement of the Telemann D Major Trumpet Concerto to the memory of the older brother of my Haïtian Leroy brothers, Hughes Leroy.

This particular piece had special meaning for me, since I had also performed it at the funerals of my birth father and several dear father-figures in my life. The melody soars higher and higher, without great changes in volume. It gives a great feeling of peace and solemnity to both the audience and performer.

On Sunday morning, I bid "au revoir"("until we meet again") to my "big brother" Gaguy Depestre, and promised to stay closely in touch (leading to tremendous phone bills before I discovered the wonderful computer program called "SKYPE" which I now use regularly for international calls).

"Tremblement" (Earthquake)

As I stood to pass out papers in the jazz band rehearsal on Tuesday, January 12th, I placed my ZN5 camera/phone next to my calendar on the piano's music stand.

Suddenly, I heard a low rumble, like an ominous timpani roll.

"Oh, no" I thought, "they've damaged a supporting column in the new construction in the elementary school and it's coming down."

That thought lasted all of two or three seconds before the floor began to buck and heave like the surface of the ocean in a hurricane, and I knew we were having an earthquake. Professor Laënnec Hurbon had predicted this the previous summer when we were in music camp at Leogane.

"Run" I shouted, then had no time for anything else but trying (unsuccessfully) to stay on my feet as the stage tilted sharply, first toward the stage right side of the building, then back toward the back wall of the stage.

I spun in a clock-wise circle and fell to my knees, and, alone with my God, curled into a fetal position on my left side.

"Okay, Lord" I said. "If this is it, if You're taking me home, I'm okay with that. Thy will be done!"

I felt strangely calm, even as chunks of concrete ceiling were falling on and all around me and the air was filled with choking dust.

People were screaming and shouting "Jesus" over and over.

The piano, at which I had been sitting moments before, was hit by a massive block of concrete, which fell just where I had been sitting. As the stage tipped toward stage right and then tilted toward the back wall, the piano rolled first sideways, then backward, down the incline.

The large panels of lights in the ceiling fell down, with upside-down U-shaped sections between them providing the safe havens that preserved our lives on the stage and in the front part of the audience.

The official reports first said that this first earthquake arrived at 4:53 pm and lasted for seventeen seconds, then that was revised to thirty-one, and finally forty-three seconds.

But for those of us who survived being inside of buildings that collapsed on and around us, time as we knew it was suspended, and the quake seemed to last forever.

All concepts of space and time disappear when solid ground becomes like jello and bucks like an angry stallion!

"Ki e la?" ("Who's here?") I shouted, anxious to know which of my students might have been hurt, and whether all or any of them had survived.

"Manmi"("Mom") said young David Saintilus, who had re-mained on stage with me and rose from the dust at the very rear of the stage, under the still hanging portrait of Ste Cecilia.

Guemali, Fleury, Pipot and Rock were at the foot of the stage.

They soon climbed up the risers toward the back of the au-ditorium, where they could see some light shining through from outside. I later learned that they climbed down on top of the roof outside the building to safety.

Young David assisted me to my feet and to the stairs at center stage, after I had retrieved my briefcase/bag (filled with dust), but

my calendar book, cell phone and water bottle were all disappeared into the dusty rubble at the back of the stage.

We moved toward the steel door off stage-left, down-stage,
noting that the orchestra pit just off the edge of the left side of the
stage had risen into what looked like a small volcano.

There was constant rumbling as more and more of the building fell.

And then the shouting and screaming began to crescendo. .
.

Aftershocks

As David and I entered the doorframe, we were joined by my god-son, Jeani Remy, and his bass teacher, Ariane Saul. Both were hysterical: their basses had been knocked violently from their hands and Jeani was bleeding profusely from a wound to his scalp.

We had just reached the doorframe, which had tilted to a 60 degree angle, when a series of strong aftershocks rocked the already precarious structure.

I calmed and hugged and blessed all three of my students.

I remember holding both Jeani and Ariane tightly in my arms and reassuring them that everything would be okay.

David scampered on his hands and knees down what had been the hallway, now ruined, to safety. I later saw him outside the cathedral, and he was a great help to me in our makeshift emergency hospital on the grounds of the ruined cathedral.

As we stood in the door frame we could hear people climbing on the roof of the auditorium.

"*Ne marchez pas!*" ("Don't walk there") we shouted, afraid that more of the ceiling would fall in upon us.

Later, we learned that it had been Pere David Cesar himself

walking on the roof, heroically leading his 5th floor office staff down to safety.

Strong tremors continued to rock us, and cause more pieces of the ceiling and balcony to fall for several more minutes.

Jeani and Ariane and I soon followed the same route as David, but I fell several times, injuring my knees and piercing my right hand on a nail.

The floor was slippery because the mortar dust was as fine as talcum powder on the tile floor and made it feel like water on the surface of ice.

Then we were finally in the hallway outside Nicole St. Victor's office. The stairs down to the elementary school were gone, as was the lunch-room/ante-chamber, and the left-side corridor into la Salle Ste. Cecile.

We moved around to the practice room side of the horseshoe. Ariane and Jeani were able to hop down six feet to the remains of what had been the Romel Joseph rehearsal room (named for the brilliant Haitian violin soloist who had returned to Haiti after studying at the Juilliard School and winning a Fulbright Scholarship for his abilities), but I didn't trust my legs to handle the drop.

I turned back to assist in breaking down a steel practice room door, behind which a piano student was trapped. Several of us took turns beating at the door with the bottoms of music stands, until the door finally gave way and the student exited.

Then I returned to the hallway outside Nicole's and Manmi Rose's offices where one of the young, mini-string students was trapped under a huge piece of concrete which had fallen from the ceiling. Her Papa tried to pull on her as first two, then three, then finally five of us, struggled to lift the heavy cement. ("*Sur quatre: une, deux, trois, quatre, POUSSEZ! (Push!)*" And finally she was free.

Protecting her beneath the concrete, saving this young girl from death and injury, was Madame Ismique Lahens, who protected her charges in death as in life. One of the parents who assisted with lifting the concrete pulled Ismique's body out onto the floor. I felt her carotid artery for a pulse, but too much time had passed since the earthquake, and she was dead. It was too late to attempt resuscitation.

"*Requiem æternam dona ei, Domine, et lux perpetua luceat ei. Requiescat in pace.*"

("Eternal rest grant unto her, oh Lord, and let perpetual light shine upon her. Rest in peace.")

I blessed her body and commended her spirit to Almighty God.

The policeman took my hand and showed me where to put my feet on the piles of rubble in the ruined stairwell. We moved across into what had been the Romel Joseph rehearsal room, which had led to the newer section of practice rooms.

At the back of this room, someone had broken a window, and people were exiting the room through that window.

I climbed onto a folding metal chair, then onto the back of that chair up into the window frame that was filled with glass shards. I had to have assistance to bend my legs enough to get through the window, because my knees were swollen from having fallen so many times that day.

Eventually, by shifting so that my back was against one side of the window, we were able to bend my legs enough to get me through.

I slid down a waiting door placed as a slide against the window, then climbed onto more slabs of concrete roofing, and finally up into the balcony hallway between the music school and the elementary school.

Skendre Desrosiers, our acting principal hornist in OPST, is a major hero. He helped me down the door-slide to exit the music school. He continued to go back and forth into the ruins all night long to lead others to safety and then worked all day with me in the little emergency hospital on the grounds of the cathedral the day after the earthquake. He also helped bring most of the items that I salvaged from the guest house back out to the parking lot of the cathedral.

Once I had accessed the second floor balcony of the elementary school, I made my way to the stairs leading down to the school playground and courtyard of the elementary school which led to the church grounds.

I kept telling myself:

"It's okay, the school fell, but the cathedral is still standing and I can go in, sit down (since I knew my knees were not ready to kneel right now) and give thanks to God and pray for guidance."

I was concerned to note that the louvered wall between the courtyard and the old auditorium had apparently fallen, and that the back of the staircase had started to fall into the staircase, spewing debris from rooms above.

But I was sure that everything would be okay when I reached the cathedral.

Everything Is Not Okay

I walked toward the gate, leading to the cathedral. Dust hung in the air, and it was turning to dusk now.

I was determined to reach the safe haven of the church.

I walked out to the parking area to find that the beautiful Holy Trinity Cathedral, home to the first pipe organ in the Caribbean, location of many beautifully executed religiously-themed murals, had fallen.

My knees buckled, and had not Pere David Cesar been there to catch me, I think I would have fallen again.

"Oh, David" I exclaimed. "It's too much: not the cathedral..."

I burst into tears and buried my head in Pere David's chest.

But only for a moment.

There was work to do: assessment of survivors and those who needed rescue, treatment for the wounded, consolation for those who were mourning and frightened, prayers and hugs—I could no longer indulge in my own misery, but must respond now to others.

Who is here? Who is missing? Had this one arrived yet for

rehearsal? That one? Had he/she gotten out safely?

Pere David...Bernadette...Ariane...Jeani Remy..("where is my little brother?")...

Nicole St.Victor...

Fleury...Pipot...Guemali...David Saintilus...Charles...Canes... Where is Dominique?

Faces became a blur through tears, yet more precious than any gift could be!

We gathered away from the school and church walls, lest they collapse with the aftershocks.

I walked out into the street (Avenue Mgr. Guilloux) to see that the Catholic Cathedral of Notre Dame had also collapsed.

My students ran after me:

"Manmi Jeanne, come back—It's Lalanne."

"Come back with us—it is not safe!"

News trickled in: the national palace, home of the president, had collapsed...the gas tanks in Carrefour had ruptured and/ or exploded...through the night we could see flames in the distance...minutes passed like hours...hours passed like days...

Would another quake hit us? When would the next aftershock turn our legs (and the ground) again to jello?

The Sisters of St. Margaret, our beloved order of Episcopalian nuns, were in the courtyard behind the ruined cathedral, with a dozen or so students from St. Vincent's School for the Handicapped.

Eventually we would all help carry these children to vans to be transported to the College St. Pierre campus, where they would live in the temporary tent city that was established on the soccer field of the ruined school campus.

Everywhere, it seemed, was another person or persons escalating into hysteria.

"Paix" I said again and again ("Peace"), as I hugged them.

"Jesu e ak ou, Jesu e ak mwen, Jesu e ak nou" (Jesus is with you, Jesus is with me, Jesus is with us).

I was humming an old lullaby that had come down through my father's family from World War I (something like an air-raid siren, but softer and lower: Sol-do, sol-do, sol-do, sol-do; sol-ti, sol-ti, sol-ti...repeated again and again.

I rocked and hummed and soothed and comforted and blessed and prayed, touching to heal, hugging and praying with and for so many all through that long night.

When I was little, I remember hearing my great grandmother speak of shooting stars as being souls going directly to heaven.

Sister Marjorie of the Sisters of St. Margaret and I spoke of the miracles that we had witnessed and would witness over that day and the succeeding days. I told her of my family's tradition about shooting stars.

"Every soul who died today will go straight to heaven" she said with confidence.

That night, the sky was filled with shooting stars, and white birds circled all around us in the parking lot of the cathedral... they were not pigeons, nor seagulls, nor bats: I had never seen anything quite like them.

I like to think that they were manifestations of the Holy Spirit, sent to guide and protect us.

On one of my many trips back into the courtyard, I saw a light on in one of the elementary school classrooms. The door was open, so I went in to investigate.

God Provides

As I entered the well-lit classroom, I assessed the available supplies, finding dozens of empty and partially filled "Tampico" and water bottles (which we eventually used in the little hospital to provide drinking water and water for taking Tylenol and Ibuprofen for our patients). Here there was a desk made of wood, with drawers that would hold supplies. There was a table that would become an examining table, chairs and benches for the weary.

Climbing up the risers to the back wall of the classroom, I found through the collapsed rear wall that the guest house appeared to be still standing.

An answer to prayer: God always provides.

Come morning light, I would return to salvage whatever I could find from the guest house.

I returned to the outer lot, to check on some of our first patients (most on planks of wood, or pieces of doors).

Here was Joey, Jeani Remy's little brother, with a badly broken leg. There was an unidentified student who'd been rescued from under the ruins of the professional school, whose lower body had been crushed beneath the rubble. His back appeared to be broken, paralyzing his lower limbs. His hands were frozen in a rictus of clawing.

There were many crushing injuries. There was a woman who could not walk, an elderly man with a crushed pelvis, waving his arms and shouting *"Jesus, m'aidez"* ("Jesus: help me")

I returned to the courtyard and grabbed a bench from outside the elementary school office.

"Godmother!" cried Jeani. "Come back. It is not safe!"

"Here, Remy" I handed him the first bench. "Take this outside."

I turned to get the other bench.

Then, after passing that off, I called to Skendre to come help me and began raiding the classrooms for anything that might be useful.

One of the elderly gatekeepers came to me to protest my removal of items from the classrooms and I'm a little ashamed to say that I became the Army drill sergeant that my father had been:

"Cette responsibilité est la mienne! Ai-je déclaré directement al'éveque, Jean Zaché!" ("The responsibility is mine. I report directly to the Bishop Jean Zaché Duracin!")

He backed away, with a salute. Later I saw him watching over me from a distance with a smile as I treated the many patients in the outer courtyard through the day on Wednesday.

At about 1 am Tuesday night, Skendre came to me.

"Manmi Jeanne" He began. "I am going back into the school and I am not coming out again unless I have Mejeun with me."

Emmanuel Mejeun was another very talented horn player in the orchestra and a dear friend of Skendre's. He had been practicing in the new practice rooms when the earthquake arrived. He was caught beneath a column that had fallen across his waist, and several people had tried unsuccessfully to lift the column and rescue him. His father was sitting with him, hoping for a miracle.

"Skendre" I embraced and blessed him and took him by the shoulders.

"I am sending St. Michael, the Archangel, with you. He will give you strength and his sword will assist you in rescuing Mannie."

In less than an hour, Skendre returned, with Mannie's arm draped over his shoulder.

Skendre (backed by St. Michael the Archangel) had lifted the pillar "with strength I had never before known" and rescued his friend.

Perhaps the aftershocks had loosened the column, enabling Skendre to lift it by himself and pull his friend to safety.

I prefer to believe that a tall, heroic angel used his sword as a fulcrum to assist Skendre.

We have the power to command angels: God provides.

Mannie was conscious, lucid, but having pains in his belly (an injured or ruptured spleen, I worried?) but didn't appear to have the symptoms of massive inflammation and bruising that so many suffered.

"*Que le bondieu te benisse*" I marked the Sign of the Cross on his forehead. "Be blessed and healed in the Name of Jesus Christ the Lord!"

This was the strongest medicine ever known: I recalled the Acts of the Apostles and the Book of Saint Peter.

I turned to find a seat and close my eyes for a minute—but only for a minute, since I could not rest. There continued to be aftershocks, both actual and reactive throughout the long night.

With the actual aftershocks, I noticed a change in air pressure so that my ears would pop, then the earth would wobble again briefly. Everyone would moan or cry "Jesu, Jesu!" and wait in abject terror to see if another quake would hit us. But none did.

Mother Gaia was just settling back down for another (long, we hoped) night of sleep.

The last one had lasted some 160 years, since the previous earthquake in Haiti had been in the 1840s, and the last one in Port-au-Prince had been in the late 1700s. She was just grumbling a bit, or clearing the phlegm from the back of her throat.

With the reactive aftershocks, it was a response of the limbic system or nervous system that spread more by suggestion:

"Did you feel that?" was all it took and everyone in the area would again describe the experience of what I came to call "jello-legs."

You could not trust your senses and it was impossible to discern whether your experience was real or stress-related. And we were all suffering from post-traumatic-stress disorder, of course.

The feeling is a bit like that of trying to walk on land after you've been on a small to medium sized sea-going vessel. Cruise ships and large boats are often so stable that you don't have the same experience.

Your stability is compromised: you wobble when you walk, and your muscles feel weak and uncoordinated. You feel the need to hold onto something solid.

And then the sensation passes and you breathe a shaky sigh of relief.

Two gentlemen from the SogeBank across the Avenue Mgr. Guilloux from the cathedral, worked hard all night long to keep the bank's generator running so that there would be a spotlight shining into the cathedral parking lot for all of us. Frantz and Philippe continued to check-in on us as well. They were a real blessing.

During that long Tuesday night, sitting vigil in the front of the ruined Ste. Trinite Cathedral, I wondered and worried about members of the jazz ensemble who had not been in the Salle Ste Cecile before the quake hit.

These included Lucannes, a brilliantly talented pianist who is legally blind; Bryce Jameson, a trombonist; Leone, a trombonist, who was due to be late, as he was coming from work in Petion Ville; Pierre Richard Etienne, a trumpeter, who was also coming from work.

But the one about whom I worried the most was my beloved friend, Professor Laënnec Hurbon, who plays the alto saxophone.

Laënnec is one of the most amazing intellectuals I've ever met. Originally planning to become a Jesuit priest, he entered a seminary at the age of 13. While he was completing his theological studies in Paris, he realized his calling lay elsewhere.

He has become a world-renown socio-anthropologist as well as a truly egalitarian humanist. He holds three doctoral degrees from the Sorbonne (theology, sociology and anthropology), has written and published 16 books and hundreds of scholarly articles. He is in demand as a featured speaker at colloquiums world-wide, particularly concerning societal development, slavery and world religions.

He is a co-founder of the acclaimed Quisqueya University of Haïti, and a director for the Center for Scientific Research in Paris.

And yet this brilliant, brilliant man, who is fluent in six languages (and reads and writes in several more), humbles himself and plays in bands with young people on a weekly basis.

Laënnec had told me on the phone at 3:40 pm that he was starting down to rehearsal.

"I will be on time" he had said to me (referring to a previous conversation about the laxity in punctuality so common in Haiti).

"*Pas de problem*" I said. "*Voyage sûr!*" ("No problem, safe journeys")

Had he arrived? Was he beneath the rubble in the staircase leading up to the music school? In the chamber that was fallen before that staircase? In the pile of rubble that covered the left-hand corridor into La Salle Ste. Cecile?

I didn't know. All through the night, the tail lights of a crushed white mini-suv had been blinking, blinking, blinking under the fallen front of the cathedral.

I was very afraid that this was my friend Laënnec's car, and that he had, indeed, arrived on-time for the rehearsal and had been caught in the collapsing staircase on his way up into the music school.

The car was parked near where Laënnec would usually park his car when attending events at the school. (I wracked my brain but couldn't remember the make or model or license plate number of his car.)

All night long, I revisited the back of that car, wondering, hoping, wishing that perhaps the windshield had protected him and that he was, in fact, alive and could be rescued from the crushed car.

The tail lights kept blinking, piercing my heart with "What ifs" and "Please, God, no..."

My heart was aching with the thought that he might or might not be in the car, that he might be lost inside the ruins of the school, that I might have lost his brilliance and kindness forever. . .

Somehow, I managed to continue to function, almost on autopilot, since I could not bear to feel the loss that was encroaching upon my sanity, moment by moment, at the thought that I had lost one of my dearest friends!

Morning Finally Arrives

Around 5 am the sun began to brighten the sky. All night long the white birds had continued to fly back and forth above us: Angels? Holy Spirit? Whatever they had been, they had been a comfort at a bad time.

"Skendre" I called. "Let's try the guest house."

We proceeded through the courtyard and entered the passageway leading to the gift shop and guest house.

There were many pieces of concrete strewn all along the way, and at the end of the passage was a broken-off metal bar from a long concrete section that had to be climbed over. Could we do so?

Yes. Okay, made it.

But now the metal gate, which had always stood open at the top of the little stairway, had fallen over and was covered with heavy chunks of cement (too heavy to be moved). The 60 degree angle formed by the door left about 30 inches of space, just shy of a meter high, so we could crouch down and crawl beneath it.

Once through that obstacle, the way was fairly clear. Around the corner and….

Yes: the guest house still stood. *Grâce au bondieu!* (Thanks be to God!)

There were many cracks in the walls around Pappy Gerard's first floor chamber, but the walls were reinforced by metal panels and stood.

I opened the gate to the stairway with my key and proceeded cautiously up the stairs. Much of the decorative cement block alongside the stairwell had fallen, either into the stairs or out, into the alleyway.

At the top of the stairs, I could see that the kitchen area was destroyed (thank God I knew Marlene had left an hour or so before the tremblement: I hoped she was okay). Debris from the professional school above had smashed through the back wall and the counter, sink and stove were all gone.

But the refrigerator was still upright in the dining room area, and it still had water (and ice) and some food inside.

There were plastic cups and dishes, folding chairs...

And in my room? Basically intact: many items had fallen to the floor (including my beloved "Celebration" trumpet: now dented by the first valve casing. The valves still moved, but I could not remove the first valve any more.)

My Toshiba laptop computer was safe on the extra bed, intact inside its protective sleeve. My medicines and vitamins and water treatment tablets were all safe in the drawers.

Now we began to pack things up to bring down and outside:

Sheets, pillows, mattresses, clothing and robes for blankets and to tear into strips for bandages/braces/slings,

A bottle of Tylenol (partial); tampons and sanitary napkins for soaking up blood and dressing wounds, a bottle of Ibuprofen; a small tube of triple antibiotic ointment (which should have been gone in an hour or less, but somehow, like the lamp in the Temple with only enough oil for one night which miraculously lasted for eight nights, lasted all day and night)

An oil lamp and matches!

And a big box, filled with supplies for my new apartment: paper towels and toilet paper, Q-tips, Lysol spray, Clorox spray, Listerine, Witch Hazel, Arid gel deodorant (aluminum zirconium—

would it help fight infection in wounds?), Special K cereal with yogurt drops (to feed the patients), and more…

Skendre and I worked tirelessly, bringing out the supplies. It was difficult to get many other folks to help because they were all in shock and dealing with various degrees of PTSD (post-traumatic-stress disorder).

But Skendre was a right arm for me.

"Skendre" I told him many times, "You are a rock. I'm going to give you a new name: you are no longer just 'Skendre' but you are now called 'Peter' the Rock!"

He laughed, but he understood the reference to Saint Peter.

I have learned a new way of asking for aid: Make a request. If the listener's heart is moved, they will respond as well as they are able. If their heart is hardened no amount of exhortation will elicit any favorable response.

This does not mean I cannot still evoke the Army drill sergeant at need.

But I have learned to make a request and then go about doing my Father's work myself, without waiting to see who or how many will join me. Some always do, eventually, especially when they see me continue to work incessantly.

All mothers know the value of a well-placed "guilt-trip."

All through the long night I had worried about my beloved friends and colleagues, students and family members here in Haiti. My phone was lost in the rubble, as was my calendar book with all my information. I wracked my brain to remember phone numbers and prayed someone would have a working cell phone so I could make calls to find out about those I loved.

I had switched off a part of my heart so that I could continue to work, but I ached with uncertainties about so many: Pierre Leroy and his family? Gaguy Depestre? Our beloved Bishop Jean Zaché? Jude and Mallory, who were here from the States and teaching at the Seminary?

And what of my family back in the US? I knew they would be frantic when they heard about the earthquake in Haiti. My mother, my son, my sister, my brothers, and my church family at Holy Trinity Armenian Apostolic Church, in Cambridge, Massachusetts: I could literally feel the strength of all of their prayers—the energy was quite palpable, granting me the strength to go on, when my body, mind and heart were exhausted.

There was no internet, limited cell phone networking, and no ability at all to make international calls.

Rumors were flying about evacuations of American citizens, but I knew I could not leave my Haiti now when she needed me!

"E.R." Ste Trinite

All through the night the sky was filled with hundreds, maybe thousands of shooting stars—beautiful to behold, especially in light of my great-grandmother's description of shooting stars being souls flying directly to Heaven.

5 am came with a slight glimmer of hopefulness that a second quake would not occur: it had been 12 hours—but it still seemed like a lifetime since that "ordinary Tuesday afternoon" became an endless Tuesday night.

And yet, here came the dawn, and the immediate, pressing demands of that day were only beginning...

To set up my "clinic" I dragged two tables close to the front gates to use as examining tables, an old wooden desk with two drawers to hold supplies, half a dozen chairs in a semi-circle around the desk.

I searched through the bags, boxes, and suitcases we'd brought down from the guest house to provide inventory for the clinic:

    3 x 120 ct. Carefree Panty Shields

    2 x 40 ct. boxes of OB tampons (to pack wounds)

1 x 3 oz. tube of triple antibiotic ointment
3 x 3 oz. partially filled bottles of Witch Hazel
1 x medium (8 oz.) bottle of Nasal Saline Solution
1 x pair of scissors (which had been stolen by noon)
2 x 3 oz. bottles of Listerine mouthwash
1 x 300 ct. q-tips
1 x 500 ml. of Barbancourt 5 star Rum
1 x roll of Bounty adjustable size paper towels
1 x 4 pack of Angel Soft toilet paper
A few safety razors
Some dental floss
1 x partially filled bottle of Tylenol Extra strength gel caps
1 x partially filled bottle of Ibuprofen
1 x can of Listerine spray
1 x bottle of Clorox bleach spray
No tape. (I will never go anywhere again without several rolls of duct tape and adhesive tape!
No anesthesia!
No mercurochrome or Merthiolate!

But wait! Here are two containers of Secret antiperspirant gel that has aluminum zirconium in it, and can be used to help prevent the growth of Athlete's foot fungus—would it also help prevent bacterial infection? Worth a try…

So the clinic opened for business.

At first, with Skendre's help, I treated just those who'd been brought, injured, out of our own schools.

There were many bruises, open wounds, scalp and facial wounds (some were very bloody, but I quickly learned to distinguish between superficial and deep injuries), orthopedic injuries such as sprained ankles (many), knees, hips, wrists, and shoulders.

Then there were a few whose injuries were far graver. I naively sent them to the "the hospital." Within a few hours they were all back: all the hospitals that still existed were inundated with many unattended patients. The living and the expired lay on the ground without anyone to give them attention.

There were so few available medical personnel: many had been lost in the collapse of hospital, clinic and office buildings in which they had served.

So my patients returned to my care.

Those with crushing injuries, in whom massive inflammation had begun, needed IV fluids and antibiotics, and treatment for shock. We had nothing to give them but prayers and kindness.

We scavenged clothing, drapes, and towels to use as blankets. We would not spare the bed sheets, as they could be ripped into strips to tie on the "Carefree panty shields" that served as wound dressing.

Without exception, I learned with time, to my great sadness, that all those with severe crushing of the full lower extremities (both legs) would die within 48 hours because we did not have the resources with which to treat them. Indeed, even with those resources, it is likely that many would have died anyway, due to shock and infection.

This was a veritable "baptism by fire" as I was fully immersed in the needs of others. The noise was overwhelming as every person was calling for help or for "Jesus" or crying out in pain. Many times family members, who had learned from previous experience to be assertive in asking for aid, were relentless in insisting that I treat their patients first. Everything was coated with the fine dust caused by the collapse of the buildings around us, and the smells of blood and excrement from the injured surrounding me were sometimes overwhelming.

I could take no heed of my own injuries until sometime Thursday afternoon when my body gave out on me and I collapsed and slept over 14 hours straight.

But there was still much to do before that could occur.

I turned back to my ragged little flock and distributed a box of Special K with Yogurt Drops in meager handfuls to each and a small drink of water from the bottles we'd salvaged from the guest house (two 5-gallon jugs, plus three buckets of bathroom water, usually used for bucket showers, which I treated with iodine tablets, of which I had three bottles, plus one bottle of chlorine drops—all left over from my first trip to Haiti—six trips and eighteen months ago, in July of '08)

I moved from patient to patient, striving to clean and cover wounds to prevent the incessant flies from laying eggs in them and causing infection or worse to occur.

Here was a young man with a puncture in his right eye: all I could do was to cover his eye with a pad and tie that around his head with a strip of cloth torn from a sheet.

"But I can't see!"

"Better to not see for a while and still have your eyes later" I advised.

I allowed myself a sip of water every so often, but declined food: I reasoned that I have sufficient stores to last for a long time in my body fat and will not take from those with no reserves.

I glanced at my watch: 6:00 am.

"Manmi Jeanne! Mejeun wants to go home!"

"No, Mannie, you must rest: you have an injured spleen and could bleed internally if you are too active. Lie down and rest!"

Where had that knowledge come from? I didn't know, but knew it was valid from the tenderness in his belly.

Marc-Philippe Guerrier, one of my trumpeters in jazz band, had a badly sprained, possibly broken ankle.

My students helped each other to rise and move to the sides of the area to relieve their bladders.

Can these be my smiling, happy children, usually laughing and joking and playing word games, and laughing at my feeble attempts to to do a "tuipé"(a Haitian way of sucking on the teeth to express disapproval)?

Who were these grim young men, moving about so surely to lend their strong arms to the needy all around them, so strong, so sure of themselves, so earnest in their desire to serve their God and their fellow beings with their "Manmi"?

I felt overwhelmed with pride and appreciation for these young ones, my gifts from God: Skendre, Jean Remy, Fleury, Carl-Henri, David Saintilus, Fritz, Pipot, Edward, Raphael, Delinois, and La-lanne (a Boy Scout whom, I learned, later joined the "busker" squads in searching for and retrieving the deceased from collapsed buildings.)

As the sun rose higher, it brought welcome warmth after the strangely cold winds that blew through the night.

Actually, this unusual cold spell is itself a blessing, for it slows the corruption of the bodies in the collapsed buildings. It is also a blessing that it is neither the rainy season, during which it would be impossible to sleep outside as so many millions are now doing, nor the blistering summer's heat, which would speed the corruptive process exponentially!

As the hours passed, more and more patients began to arrive at the gates, seeking treatment from the "medicin" (doctor) they had heard was at Ste. Trinite.

But I am not a "doctor" or nurse, just a music teacher with a heart and a calling to serve!

Yet still they came.

I had 6 chairs and 2 tables surrounding me and each was filled with a severely wounded patient, and the line behind each was 5 or 6 people deep with many, many more out on the street, clamoring to get in.

"Premiere les ti-mouns" ("first the children") I attempted to triage: to evaluate the most serious cases, to establish treatment priorities, but for hours at a time there was scarcely a chance to breathe!

I am fair-skinned, blond with green eyes, and must be careful about sun-exposure. Yet this day, I would sit in direct sun for 12 hours. Though I could feel myself burning by mid-day, I had no sunscreen, nor any way to shield myself from the sun—and no time to worry about taking breaks, either!

Inspiring Patients

It was very inspiring to see the courage of the many young children, so many of them with grave injuries, who accepted treatment without crying out, even as tears streamed down their sad, cement-covered little cheeks.

"*Ou gen courage*" ("You are brave") I told them.

"*Je suis fier de toi*" ("I am proud of you")

I would gently touch their cheeks and bless them and pray for their healing in the Name of Jesus Christ of Nazareth, and their eyes would shine!

These, I knew, were the great hope of Haiti and must be cherished and nurtured with tender, loving care.

At the same time, I was dismayed by the (thankfully relatively small) number of whining adults with relatively minor injuries who complained bitterly and incessantly.

"*Gadé ti-moun yo*" I would admonish them. ("Look at the children")

And that usually was sufficient to stop their complaints.

Haitians do love their children with a passion that is wonderful to see—and it extends to all children in a whole and healthy way, except in the sad cases of the *Rest-aveks*, which is an institution of a type of slavery that I hope never rises again from the ruins of the city.

Because many Haitians are Catholic, birth-control measures are limited, and often non-existant. Thus, many poor families in the provinces are unable to care for all of their children. They will make an arrangement with wealthier family members or acquaintances in the city to take in one or more of their children.

These hosts will pay the original family some money and promise to feed, clothe and educate the young children in their care.

Sadly, in many cases these children work from before dawn until late evening. They often are not well-fed, receive no additional clothing, are not allowed to attend school, and serve as slave labor to the household. If they object, or fail to complete their duties to the satisfaction of their hosts, they are beaten for being unappreciative of the "privileges" they have received.

Those who run away from their masters will live on the street, resorting to begging and prostitution. They become ill, often are HIV-positive, and become alcoholic or drug addicted because alcohol and drugs may be cheaper than food.

Many of the children who came into the clinic had severe scalp wounds, with pieces of cement embedded in the sides. I had no tweezers with which to debride these wounds, but disinfected them with nasal saline solution, covered them with a dab of triple antibiotic ointment and a pad and tied them up with a strip of cloth.

This brought a sort of flashback experience and I knew the frustrations of field medics in long-ago wars, who faced the same sorts of insufficiencies in their attempts to treat their patients. At least we now had some understanding of infection and were attempting to prevent it!

Many of the wounded were also suffering from gross lacerations of the hands or feet, especially those who had been wearing only flip-flop sandals when the earthquake arrived or as they exited ruined buildings.

With each and every patient, when I finished doing whatever I could (or could not) do for them, I would make the Sign of the Cross on their forehead *"Que le bondieu te benisse"* ("God bless you") and "Be blessed and healed in the Name of Jesus Christ, the Lord!"

For the most severe injuries, in which the lacerations extended down to where I could see tendons and bones exposed, I would also cross myself and pray for strength and wisdom before proceeding.

For those with obviously broken bones, I advised that the patients be brought to a hospital for x-rays. Though I eventually realized this to be a futile hope, I felt it fostered a thread of normalcy for the patients and those who had brought them into our little clinic. At least, I hoped it did so.

In retrospect, I think I could have tried to set and brace some of the breaks with pieces of wood from the ruins and strips of cloth. But that would have been very time consuming and exhausting of the limited human resources we had available.

Plus, we had no painkillers to treat the patients, either during or after the process (and they would have needed narcotics, especially for those with compound fractures, for whom I could not be sure the bones were properly aligned. Moving those severely broken bones could also have jeopardized veins and arteries).

So I made the difficult choice to compartmentalize and prioritize those who would and would not be treated.

Yet I could not entirely dispense with compassion: I knowingly and willingly gave Tylenol to those whom I knew were dying in the hopes that it would ease their way somewhat.

"First do no harm"

Wasn't that a part of the Hippocratic Oath that doctors took?

"I swear by Apollo, the healer, Asclepius, Hygieia, and Panacea, and I take to witness all the gods, all the goddesses, to keep according to my ability and my judgment, the following Oath and agreement: To consider dear to me, as my parents, him who taught me this art; to live in common with him and, if necessary, to share my goods with him; To look upon his children as my own brothers, to teach them this art. I will prescribe regimens for the good of my patients according to my ability and my judgment and never do harm to anyone. I will not give a lethal drug to anyone if I am asked, nor will I advise such a plan; and similarly I will not give a woman a pessary to cause an abortion. But I will preserve the purity of my life and my arts. I will not cut for stone, even for patients in whom the disease is manifest; I will leave this operation to be performed by practitioners, specialists in this art. In every house where I come I will enter only for the good of my patients, keeping myself far from all intentional ill-doing and all seduction and especially from the pleasures of love with women or with men, be they free or slaves. All that may come to my knowledge in the exercise of my profession or in daily commerce with men, which ought not to be spread abroad, I will keep secret and will never reveal. If I keep this oath faithfully, may I enjoy my life and practice my art, respected by all men and in all times; but if I swerve from it or violate it, may the reverse be my lot." ("The Hippocratic oath: text, translation and interpretation" By Ludwig Edelstein Page 56 ISBN 978-0801801846 (1943)

I tried, very hard, to honor this as best I could.

And I blessed and touched and prayed for healing for each and every person I encountered.

Injuries and Treatments

This chapter describes in detail the injuries I observed and treated at Ste. Trinite the evening and day following the first earthquake.

The first injuries were in victims from the Ste. Trinite schools/community itself.

DEATHS

Unfortunately, there were a number of deaths.

First was Madame Ismique Lahens, who collected the identification cards from all students who entered the music school each day. We discovered her body when we rescued a child who had been partially trapped under a huge piece of concrete, but survived. Then it became clear that Madame Lahens' body had cushioned the child.

Ismique was limp, with no visible injuries, no respiration, and no pulse. Resuscitation could not be attempted since it had been more than 30 minutes since the collapse. Even in death, she served as a *"Protectrix"* ("protector") of the children. Approximate time of death: 5 pm, 12 January, 2010, mostly likely due to a blow to the base of the skull.

Second: the young student who'd been rescued from the electrical school and had an apparently broken spine. He had some use of his hands/arms, but they were some sort of rictus when he was first brought out from the rubble, and he had no sensation or movement in his lower body at all. He slipped into Cheynes-Stokes breathing and died mid-afternoon on Wednesday, 13 January, approximately 2 pm, from massive trauma.

Third: an elderly man brought in on board, with a crushed pelvis and bleeding in the groin. He died late Wednesday afternoon, most likely from shock. Time of death 4:30 pm 13 January, 2010.

Fourth: a young woman, aged approximately mid-30's, had the massive crushing injuries to her lower body, with resulting edema. She died approximately 2:30 pm, 13 January, 2010, from massive trauma/shock.

Fifth: a young man, in his early 20's, was brought in on a board, lying on his belly, writhing in pain, and covered with liquid excrement and blood. Upon examination he was found to have an extremely deep laceration, to the pelvic bone in the right side of his groin, from which blood was spurting. He died approximately 15 minutes later, from severe blood loss and shock.

Sixth: a young woman, another victim of crushing injuries, died by the gates to the Ste. Trinite playground, at about 12:30 pm, 13 January, 2010, from blood loss and shock.

Seventh: a young girl, with a huge swelling on her head. Her eyes were clouded and non-responsive. She lay, limp, in her father's arms, and died at 3 pm, 13 January, 2010, from concussion.

Eighth: (at College Ste. Pierre Wednesday night) Michee, a first grade teacher was rescued from the rubble at College Ste. Pierre approximately 8 pm Wednesday evening and brought to the college at about 9 pm.

Upon examination she was found to be cold to the touch, non-responsive to speech or pain, eyes open and blinking, but otherwise non-responsive. Legs were full of edema, and the left thigh had split open, displaying a deep laceration into the inner muscle and fascia (distinct layers of tissue were visible: epidermis, fatty tissue, fascia and muscle).

I dressed the wound and had her brought into the yard of the camp and ordered additional blankets to cover her and reverse the coldness (caused by shock and blood loss).

Although her temperature did rise to near-normal again, she developed severe hemorrhaging from the nose, mouth and eyes and died at 10:00 pm 13 January, 2010 from massive trauma.

Based on experience with these patients, I had small to no hope for others I had seen with similar crushing trauma to the lower extremities. I suspect that many more than these eight perished from this massive trauma over the next 24 hours but have no data to confirm this.

CRUSHING INJURIES

In every case, crushing injuries showed gross inflammation of the tissues affected: a shiny surface, with skin stretched tightly and often the "shearing" of the outer layers of skin, exposing melatonin-less tissues with frequent splitting open of the skin, as is seen, for example, in the flesh of a fire-roasted pig.

In fact, in the earlier part of the day, I attributed some of these injuries to what I thought were "burns" though I didn't understand quite how such "burns" could have occurred.

I soon came to understand, from the descriptions of rescuers, that these were, in fact, due to crushing and scraping by heavy pieces of fallen buildings.

There had been at least 2 dozen with similar injuries to Michee's, most in lesser degrees than hers, but of course, I had seen them earlier in the day and their injuries/trauma may have progressed as hers had through the succeeding hours.

I have been told by physicians that such crushing of muscles releases a toxin (myoglobin) that travels through the body and causes a shut-down of major organs, especially the kidneys, which leads to the massive edema I had seen. This is called "rhabdomyolysis," according to the Centers for Disease Control and Prevention.

Crush injuries and crush syndrome are common following entrapment in a structural collapse.

Crush injury is "compression of extremities or other parts of the body that causes muscle swelling and/or neurological disturbances". Lower extremity injuries account for most crush injuries (74%), with injuries to the upper extremities (10%), and torso (9%) are less typical.

(Centers for Disease Control and Prevention (CDC) http://www.bt.cdc.gov/masscasualties/blastinjury-crush.asp

Crushing lasting more than 1 hour and/or sudden release of a crushed body part can cause the syndrome which includes rhabdomyolysis, a condition in which crushed muscles break down and release toxic muscle cell components into the blood resulting in kidney failure, heart rhythm abnormalities, metabolic abnormalities, and other organ dysfunctions.

(Robert N. Reddix Jr., Robert A. Probe, Crush syndrome presenting three days after injury, Injury Extra, Volume 35, Issue 10, October 2004, Pages 73-75, ISSN 1572-3461, DOI: 10.1016/j.injury.2004.05.027. (http://www.sciencedirect.com/science/article/B7CRN-4CT5YWS-1/2/b0213b1dd1f037550884d-0482ca99fb9)

When infections or other medical conditions complicate crush-related kidney failure, the mortality rate is near 55%.

Best practices for crush injuries in the field prehospital including providing intravenous fluids (IV) before releasing the crushed body part, especially if entrapment has been longer than 4 hours. Failure to recognize and treat Crush Syndrome is common, especially during rescue efforts by non-medical personnel, and typically increases the death rate.

Hussain, H.C. Kwak, I. Pallister, Crush syndrome: A comprehensive surgical strategy improves

outcomes, Injury Extra, Volume 38, Issue 4, April
2007, Pages 111-112, ISSN 1572-3461, DOI:
10.1016/j.injury.2006.12.054.   http://www.sci-
encedirect.com/science/article/B7CRN-4N4JNPB-
12/2/1d74c6b122866766cf9b64a89900514e)

More information on the "crushing injury" can be found in the
following resources on the internet:

http://www.mediccom.org/public/tadmat/train-
ing/NDMS/crush.pdf (this is an excellent PDF
format article by a physician who explains the
entire situation clearly, with historical precedents
as well as treatment protocols.)

http://www.bt.cdc.gov/disasters/earthquakes/
crush.asp

http://m.acep.org/MobileArticle.
aspx?id=46079&coll_id=577&parentid=740
(American College of Emergency Physicians)

http://www.doctorswithoutborders.org/news/ar-
ticle.cfm?id=4229&cat=voice-from-the-field

http://en.wikipedia.org/wiki/Rhabdomyolysis

http://www.fireengineering.com/index/articles/
display/271535/articles/fire-engineering/vol-
ume-159/issue-9/features/prehospital-man-
agement-of-crush-injuries.html

SPRAINS AND BREAKS

There were many, many (dozens) of injuries to feet, ankles,
knees, wrists, hands and arms, in terms of obviously torn liga-
ments and broken bones.

I saw perhaps 8-10 persons with compound fractures (of
feet, legs, arms and one particular child with a huge swelling on
her forehead as well as a fracture of her thigh bone (femur) that

showed points of bone pressing through the flesh. I begged her grandmother to bring her to a hospital, but the grandmother was in denial.)

Of the ankle breaks and sprains, there seemed to be about equal numbers of inward twists and outward twists. These, I suspect, came post-quake from trying to hurry across grossly uneven surfaces which were slick from the powdery nature of the dissolved mortar in the crumbled cement.

This also seemed the case with broken or sprained wrists and some cleanly broken toes and fingers. There were also many, many foot injuries due to so many having worn "flip-flop" sandals which give no protection to the feet.

Out of the 300 or so patients I saw across Tuesday evening and Wednesday, perhaps 3 dozen (or about 10%) fell into the categories of simple breaks or sprained limbs.

HEAD INJURIES

The vast majority of those I treated had wounds of the face or the scalp (probably more than 100, or about 35-40%). Of these, there were many varieties of wounds. With infants, children, elderly, and quite a few adults, the injuries were actual scalping or shearing of the hair and scalp, always deep, and in several dozen cases the white of the bone of the skull was clearly exposed in the wounds.

There were also many, many lacerations of the forehead, cheeks and eyes, two punctured eyeballs (one had flattened and was oozing blood and viscous material), and many torn and bitten through lips.

Although I saw no severed tongues, it would not have surprised me to learn of that type of injury.

In these head wounds, of course, bleeding was copious. I was grateful to learn, upon cleansing wounds, that some that bled a great deal were only superficial (and I could have closed them with butterfly strips or super glue if those had been available).

In some cases it looked as if actual scoops of tissue had been removed completely as if by a slightly flattened melon ball tool. Many of these wounds had already formed a sort of protective coating on the surface by the time I saw the patient.

In some cases, especially in children, the borders of the wounds were crusted with cement rubble. Although I disinfected these wounds and covered them, I had no means with which to debride them of the cement pieces.

In the cases of children and infants, often their tears had combined with the mortar dust to form a solid crust across the skin. In early cases I tried to remove this, in later cases I judged it might be protective and only treated bleeding areas.

I also saw many deep lacerations of the trunk, chiefly the upper abdomen and lower back, although there were also many groin and buttock injuries.

A part of me could detach and observe the many layers of different types of tissues displayed within the wounds with interest while my hands were busy cleaning and covering the wounds, and my mouth was praying and consoling the patients and their attending family members or friends.

I saw many, many head contusions. In each case I advised the patient and family members to keep the patient awake for 24 hours (to guard against coma in case of concussion). In most cases I could not adequately evaluate the state of concussion present (due to the bright sunlight which prevented checking the eyes separately). However, in several cases a dulling of the eyes, flat or no responses, and large swellings on the head led me to strong suspicion of concussion.

The simplest test, of checking equal pupil response to light, was unavailable due to our being out-of-doors in bright sunlight.

GROSS LACERATIONS

By far the greatest numbers of injuries were to extremities: hands and feet and fingers and toes.

Most were deep lacerations into the palm of the hand or sole of the foot (as if chopped into by a meat cleaver or machete).

Oddly, many of these were very clean on the edges and went so deep that they displayed the various layers of the tissues: skin, fatty tissue, tendons (connected sometimes, sometimes partially severed, and in a couple of cases, completely severed so that the distal part of the hand was hanging only by the flesh beyond the separated bones).

Many of these could, perhaps, have benefitted from suturing, but because I had no means to stitch their wounds, I fear those patients with these injuries will eventually face amputation of the affected limbs. A grace of sorts is that I seldom saw the same degree of this injury on both hands or both feet of the same person.

Often these injuries were accompanied by the crushing bruises on upper areas of the same limb or a lower/upper opposite limb. Thus, if the right hand were lacerated/partially amputated, often the right upper arm or leg showed the crushing injuries.

STOCKING AND DEGLOVING INJURIES

Another injury which was really bizarre was that of a shearing of the skin of the extremities. This left patients with very dark skin tone appearing to have large sections of skin that appeared to be Caucasian in color. At the distal part of the limb the sheared skin was gathered into what looking liked bunched nylon hose (stockings).

The following quotation, by Dr. Stephen M Schroeder, DPM, Chief of Podiatric Foot and Ankle Surgery, Southwest Washington Medical Center and Coauthor(s): Peter Blume, DPM, Director of Diabetic Foot Surgery, Department of Orthopedics, Yale New Haven Hospital; Clinical Assistant Professor, Department of Podiatric Surgery, Yale University School of Medicine describes degloving injuries of the foot, and is taken from a website: http://emedicine.medscape.com/article/1237208-overview

Degloving injuries

Degloving injuries occur due to a shearing

force on the skin, causing it to be undermined and elevated through the subcutaneous plane. A flap of tissue is created with a margin remaining intact or becoming completely avulsed. This represents a potentially serious situation that can lead to significant infection.

Initial treatment consists of high-pressure irrigation and debridement of all necrotic tissue. The soft tissue defect is similar to a burn wound; thus, common pathogens can be expected. Because these wounds on the feet typically occur in contaminated environments such as motor vehicle accidents or farm-type injuries, anaerobic pathogens also should be expected.

As with burn injuries, topical and systemic antibiotics should be administered. If a tissue flap remains intact, it is replaced over the wound and allowed to demarcate. Once the margins are defined, the nonviable tissue is debrided, and plans for final reconstruction using split-thickness skin graft or flap coverage are initiated.

I saw this injury mostly in middle-aged or older women and men, never on children or infants. I think it may have occurred from being pulled or dragged to safety from under heavy debris.

Finally, I saw many, many fingers and toes with sections of skin "pinched" away from the bone and hanging. I also saw many fingers and toes hanging from pieces of flesh (virtual amputations).

TREATMENT PROCEDURES

For all injuries, the first step was visual examination, and if available, verbal report from patient and/or family members (often accompanied by gestures).

The second step was disinfection of wounds, using Clorox or Listerine or Lysol spray (unfortunately painful, but effective) on adults and saline solution on infants and children.

The third step was application of either triple antibiotic oint-

ment (in the children's wounds), or Secret antiperspirant/deodor-
ant gel (as a protectant/astringent).

The fourth step was to apply a dressing to the wound, usually a
"Carefree" panty shield, attached by tying a strip of cloth around
the limb or head.

Next, if applicable, was the fashioning of a sort of "sling" from
strips of cloth to suspend the hand or arm from the neck.

This was followed by verbal aftercare instructions, a verbal
and hands-on blessing and prayer for healing (Apostolic, from the
Acts of the Apostles and the book of Peter: "In the Name of Jesus
Christ of Nazareth, be blessed and healed completely in mind,
body and spirit!")

At last, the patient could be discharged into the care of family
or friends, if available. If no one was available, the patient could
stay with us at Ste. Trinite.

By the end of the day Wednesday, only six patients remained
uncollected by family or friends.

Retrospective on Needs

There was so much more that could have been done, had we but had sufficient and appropriate supplies:

1. Suture kits: many hands, feet, fingers and toes could have been saved and many lacerations repaired with these.
2. Super glue: smaller lacerations and facial injuries with flaps of skin could have been closed with this.
3. Peroxide: would have made debriding possible and cleansing wounds more effective and less painful.
4. Betadine: same as peroxide, plus better disinfection
5. More triple anti-biotic ointment: would have been able to use on all patients, not just children
6. Tape: adhesive, even duct tape would have helped to better secure dressings
7. Latex or vinyl gloves (I kept washing my own hands in Clorox, but would have been able to be even more proactive with gloves, particularly in cases that required debriding)

8. Tweezers or small forceps: to debride wounds and assist in closure for suturing
9. Topical anesthetic
10. Children's aspirin: even for adults, to prevent blood
    clots from forming.

Pain of Loss

It is those for whom I could do nothing other than pray who haunt me still.

One child stands out particularly in my memory and haunts me: her grandmother had brought her into the clinic sometime in the early afternoon. She was a beautiful little girl of 9 years of age, but her eyes were already dull with shock.

She had suffered a massive, compound fracture of her femur (thigh bone) and had a huge bump on her forehead, with a probably concussion.

I advised her grandmother that she needed x-rays and a cast on her leg.

"*Li pa cassé* (It's not broken)" her grandmother exclaimed. "*Ou kapab range li* (You can fix it.)"

They remained in the yard for much of the rest of the day. Each time I passed I would bless the child and pray for her healing.

But I have small hopes that the child will survive intact. Besides the PTSD from which we will all suffer for a long time, there may be brain damage for her, and the odds are great that she will eventually lose her leg.

And sadly, this world is not kind to the handicapped, of any type.

By late morning we had dozens and dozens of patients lying on pallets or boards or directly on the ground around the yard.

These were more severe injuries: many had the severe crushing of the lower limbs with the requisite massive inflammation and split and gaping wounds that exposed inner layers of flesh, fatty deposits, muscles and sometimes bone.

Inevitably, these injuries portended imminent death. Several persons died during the morning and afternoon from these very injuries.

An extremely emaciated and elderly man arrived on a slab of wood. Naked, he had a crushed pelvis. I brought a nightgown to cover him. I blessed him and gave him Tylenol.

Each time I passed his pallet, his eyes would meet mine and he would tug the covering aside and point at his crushed pelvis almost as if it were a great, private joke between the two of us. I gave him Tylenol and blessed him and prayed over him in vain.

(As I write this, a wind-up radio is playing "There is a Balm in Gilead" I cannot stop the tears from flowing...)

His eyes closed for the last time in the mid-afternoon.

"Rest in peace and may perpetual light shine upon you!"

Jean Remy, my godson, beckoned me over to the side of the student brought out the night before from the collapsed professional school.

At my bequest, they had taken him to the national hospital, but had returned because it was impossible to enter the collapsed and overwhelmed hospital for diagnosis or treatment.

"Godmother, he is having trouble breathing."

Another of the kids was jiggling the boy's belly, trying to help.

I drew near, dread filling me to the back of my throat.

It was Cheynes-Stokes respiration—I recognized it from the experience I gained when my grandmother had died.

"*Cherie*" I began gently. "*Li alé. Dites au-revoir.*" ("My dear, he is going. Say good-bye.")

I blessed him and did a form of extreme unction (without

oil), making the Sign of the Cross over his eyes, his nostrils, his mouth.

By the time I reached his heart, the breaths stopped completely. I checked for a pulse (none) and gently closed his now-still eyes.

I turned and embraced Remy briefly, but only briefly, because his little brother was also injured and I had more patients to treat, and more arriving every minute.

Photographers came, with still and video cameras. I held up my hands:

"*S'il vous plait! Respecte!*" ("Please! Respect the patients!)

"No pictures!"

I did not want my face shown: my work was between me, my patients and my God.

Later, I realized that a photo might have reached my family in the States and reassured and comforted them, but at the actual moment, I was single-mindedly pursuing my purpose and that was to help as many as possible.

"Manmi Jeanne, may I go?" Skendre Desrosiers called. "I would like to know if my family is safe."

How could I deny this brave young man, this "Rock", my "Peter" the chance that he might find his family alive and well in La Plaine?!?

"*Voyage avec les anges. Que les anges te gardent et que le bon Dieu te benisse!*" ("Travel with the angels. May the angels guard you and God bless you.")

I embraced him and turned back to my work.

"We need more bandages. Please rip some more sheets!"

I exhorted David Saintilus who had returned to assist me.

"Jeanne!" I turned to find Jeobaham Jean-Pierre, our percussion teacher and instrument/equipment manager for the school, reaching to embrace me.

"*Grâce au bon Dieu tu vas bien!*" I repeated my mantra (Thanks be to God that you are okay!)

I traced the Sign of the Cross on his forehead and blessed him, then turned back to my work.

"You Call Yourself a 'Doctor'!"

At about 1 pm or so, as I was examining yet another patient with the horrific skin-peeling type of wounds that made it look like they had a rolled up nylon stocking at their ankle or wrist (which was actually their skin that had been stripped from the meat and bones), a woman a few people back from one of the chairs that surrounded me became angry at how long it was taking to receive treatment for the person she had brought in.

"You call yourself a 'doctor'" she clearly exclaimed, in English.

"No" I replied. "I am not a doctor, nor a nurse. I am only a music teacher, trying to help as best I can with almost nothing."

The tears came.

David translated for the crowd.

"J'ai besoin que tu pries le bon Dieu Jesus Christ pour moi." (I wish you to pray for me to the Lord Jesus Christ.)

The woman's eyes grew big and she nodded.

I stood and made my way through the throngs of people grasping at me and calling for help to the inner courtyard/playground of the school.

I sat down on a little wall, and facing the statue of a sister holding a child, I wept and prayed:

"Dear Lord, I have nothing left to give. My strength is gone. I have nothing left. You have to do this for me. I place it all in Your Hands. In Jesus' Holy Name I ask and pray."

I bowed my head briefly, then stood and returned to work.

No Help Coming

At this point in the day, several ambulances and emergency vehicles had passed by the complex. We called out to each one, to try and stop them to help us, but none would stop or even slow down.

The sun beat down mercilessly on my head. I took some money out of my fanny bag, 1000 HTGs (about $25. US) and asked a couple of students to go out and find me some orange soda and some Coca Cola to drink.

More than an hour later they returned with three glass bottles of Coke (only) and handed me the change. It was all they could find.

I drank one bottle myself, ate four pieces of cashews and gave the rest away to my student helpers. I remained determined to eat very little, but I must not become dehydrated or I would risk collapse and not be able to continue my work.

A middle-aged white man with a camera around his neck stopped by the gate.

"You must be exhausted" he said.

"I am."

"It must be overwhelming to be the only doctor with so many."

"I'm not a doctor. I'm a music teacher in the States."

"Don't you have rubber gloves?"

"At this point, what does it matter? These are matters of life and death!"

"I'm a respiratory therapist in the States."

"Great! Then come and join us and help!"

Smiling, he shook his head, put his hands up in the air and backed away, never to return.

I sighed and turned back to my duties.

While digging through the supplies we had brought down from the guest house, I came upon the book my friend Laënnec Hurbon had given me in September. Somehow this gave me a faint hope that he might have survived.

At least I hoped and prayed so.

More Patients (and more, and more)

By this time, I was surrounded by 4 or 5 very tiny little children and a couple of babies. Each had head injuries and scalp lacerations, several had large swellings on their heads.

I did what I could to assess their responsiveness: engage their eyes, talk about *"le grand boum-boum"* (the big boom-boom/ earthquake), touch them to ascertain skin tone and body temperature (to gauge level of shock).

I cleansed and dressed their wounds, blessed them and prayed over them and discharged them to their parents, warning the parents to keep the children awake for at least 24 hours to guard against their slipping into a coma from a possible concussion.

I then treated several more whining adult women, mostly with minor injuries (it seemed the more minor the injuries, the more major was the whining!), and a few whining men.

Then I faced a father with an absolutely beatific little boy of about 3 years of age (judging from his teeth).

"Wilson" had a severe laceration across the palm of his hand. I cleansed the wound, patted it gently with triple anti-biotic ointment, covered it with a sanitary napkin, and tied up the hand with strips of sheet.

Before I blessed him and consecrated him with the Apostolic prayer of healing, I gently told him:

"*Tu es un hero! Je suis si fier de toi.*"("You are a hero. I am <u>so</u> proud of you.")

His big, beautiful eyes shining, he nodded. His father, tears streaming down his cheeks said "Thank-you" and "May God bless you!" in English.

"He does, all the time" I replied, and returned to my work.

More Haunting Memories

Several young men brought in a patient who was writhing in pain and lying on his belly, but had no visible injuries, other than the fact that his bowels had given way.

He was wearing nothing but jockey shorts and had probably been about to shower (Haitians are very clean and will bathe twice or more per day when able to do so) when the earthquake happened.

His friends rolled him over and pulled aside his jockeys, exposing a deep, gaping laceration in his groin, with a pulsing, dark red blood stream.

I knew there was nothing to be done, but still blessed and consecrated him. Within 10 minutes he had rolled back over onto his belly and died.

For some time he lay on the grass between the gate and the dead and broken school. I could not reach him to close his staring eyes and the memory of those sad, staring eyes continues to haunt me.

Other things haunt me, too

For example, when I first entered the guest house and was

yelling directions to Skendre who was helping me, there came knocking from two different directions in the collapsed professional school. One sound came from the right side as I faced the ruined kitchen, the other from higher up on the left side.

"*M'ap vini*" (I'm coming) I shouted and they rapped more energetically.

I talked some young boys into climbing out onto the rubble, but there was no way through, no way to reach the knockers.

By my second or third trip into the guest house, the rapping had stopped on the right side and considerably weakened on the left side.

Late Wednesday afternoon, a group of four men who had a boy in the electrical program at the professional school arrived, hoping to find him.

I told them about the rapping, and brought them to the guest house. They called and called and called, even calling out specific names, but no response came...

They left, bemoaning the lack of a hack-saw and propane torch with which they might have been able to cut into the concrete.

After they left, I went in to use the toilet, which caused the door to squeak loudly. As I opened the door, I heard the rapping again, fainter and fainter, and fainter...

By the time I returned to the guest house on Friday morning, after I had collapsed on Thursday afternoon, there was no more rapping.

I hear that rapping in my dreams and I am just as helpless now as I was then.

"*M'ap vini*" ("I'm coming").

How many, many times had I spoken that phrase over the past 24 hours...and always followed through on that promise.

After all, there is a Haitian proverb that says "*Promesse cé dette.*" (a promise is an obligation, a debt which must be paid)

There is a Haitian word game, played when someone asks "*Promesse?*" and someone else responds "*Cé dette*" which does not mean that they have given a promise, merely that they have completed the proverb.

To get a Haitian to honor a promise, you must get them to say *"Je te promets"* ("I promise")

Well, that *"M'ap vini"* promise to the rappers can never be paid, and it will haunt me to the rest of my days.

There was a group of several young children, babies really, lying on the ground near the fence, who did not appear to be injured, but very sickly. They all had poor skin tone, little muscle tone, cloudy eyes, swollen bellies and very skinny arms and legs and very weak cries.

I brought them the remains of a pizza and some chicken fingers that had been in the guest house refrigerator. They ate ravenously, and I wondered how long it had been since the last time they had eaten, where were their parents, and who had brought them to us.

Shadrac, also called "Bebi", a deaf-mute young man who is a gifted carpenter and works at Ste. Trinite and for the summer camp at Leogane, arrived at the clinic Wednesday afternoon.

He sat and waited so patiently as I treated others. Then, when I finally reached him, removed his left shoe to expose his horrifically sprained and swollen ankle.

I gave him Ibuprofen (which I reserved for those patients who did not have bleeding injuries), and used several strips of cloth, tied together, to bind up his ankle and his foot.

I made him put his foot up and gave him the rest of a bottle of Pepsi-Cola someone had given me.

Now I turned to find Michee Charlot calling me. Michee was a clarinet and saxophone teacher at Ste Trinite and played in the OPST and the jazz ensemble. He was also my friend Laënnec Hurbon's saxophone teacher.

"Oh, Michee!" I cried. "I think Laënnec is dead!"

"Oh, no! I'm so sorry!"

He embraced me as I led him over to the car with the blinking lights (now very faint).

"That is not Laënnec's car" he said, confident.

"Are you sure?" I queried, hope beginning to rise again.

"Yes, I'm sure" he said.

"Thank God! But I still have no word of him. He did not make it to jazz ensemble, even though he said he was coming down at a little before 4 pm"

"I'm sure he is all right" Michee said, "But no one has seen or heard from Rico."

Rico Jean was my conducting student, who directed the palace band in which Michee played.

"He was not at the palace when the earthquake came, and no one has any news of him."

"Please let me know when you hear anything"

"I will. I promise."

And Michee turned to go back to his work at the palace.

"We salute you!"

At about this time, after I'd done a walk-about and distributed Tylenol to our 6 remaining patients, a member of the national press arrived and interviewed me with the help of one of the waiting parents who spoke both English and Kreyol.

I told him about the collapse of the school buildings, the rescue efforts, and our feeble little clinic that had treated over 300 patients this day with such limited supplies.

He said to me, in Kreyol, "We of the National Press salute you for what you are doing! We love and respect you!"

I asked him *"Ou gen nouvel Kompè Filo?"* (Do you have any news of Kompè Filo?)

Kompè Filo was my friend (and trumpet student) from Tele Ginen Radio/TV. The reporter told me that Kompè Filo had survived and was fine and well.

I asked him to bring my affection to Kompè Filo and received a promise that he would do so.

By now, all but our 6 bed-ridden patients had departed, mostly to Champ de Mars, the open park area near the national palace (with statues of historic figures, multiple levels, benches, lighting and a band-stand) which had become a sea of humanity.

One last little group arrived at dusk: a father with 2 teen-aged children (a boy and a girl) and a tiny little baby boy in his arms. He had rescued his son from the dead mother's arms in the rubble that had been their home, now fallen.

The infant could not be more than 2 months old, still responsive to a cheek stroke with a nursing response.

I examined him with care: no injuries, just dirt and debris in his hair and on his body. I cleaned him tenderly and gently advised his Dad that they would need a wet nurse for the child.

The father looked around helplessly, and hopeless.

"Attendez!" (Wait!) I said.

I searched through nearby boxes and found a carton of milk (2 % fat, but it would have to do)—the kind that does not require refrigeration until opened.

I grabbed the nearly empty bottle of nasal saline mist, popped the nipple and emptied it. Then I filled the bottle with milk and replaced the nipple-like tip.

I stroked the baby's cheek and gently inserted the nipple into his mouth, gently squeezing the bottle to squirt a little stream of milk into his mouth.

He nursed hungrily and his father almost smiled.

After the baby had taken about half the bottle, I had his father burp him. Success!

I covered the nipple with the bottle cap, and handed the rest of the half-gallon of milk to the father.

I blessed and consecrated each of them: father, son, daughter and baby son, and gave thanks to God for this little miracle of hope at the end of a very hard day.

Bishop's Call

Now it was close to 8 pm, and I heard someone call my name:

"*Madame Jeanne!*"

"*Oui, c'est moi*" I replied.

"Sorel is here with his *voiture* (car). The bishop is at College St. Pierre and is calling for you to come there with the sisters and the priests and the students."

"I can't leave my patients! What if the rains come? They need protection."

My godson, Jean Remy, spoke again.

"I will stay and watch over them from this car with these other three."

He pointed to his sister and two other students.

"We will put them in the tents (2 pup tents salvaged from the guest house) and we will take turns sleeping in the car."

"Okay" I said, exhaustion starting to apply, and gathered my laptop bag, my trumpet case, my gym bag (into which I placed some remaining supplies) and my fanny pack.

I got into the truck and Sorel placed my bags in the back. We traveled through the Champ de Mars, past the once- beautiful palace, now crumbled and fallen, to the entrance of College Ste. Pierre.

Empty.

All windows darkened. The right side of the building completely collapsed.

Sorel and Raphael banged on the gates and someone appeared and told them to go around to the back entrance, near the seminary.

We re-entered the truck and went around the large, ruined block to the back entrance of the college. Where the soccer field had been, there was now a refugee city, with real and makeshift tents, and many, many, many people.

The seminary buildings had all cracked and/or fallen so everyone was sleeping outside on the (occasionally) solid ground. At this point, aftershocks were a bit less harsh, a bit less frequent, but we were all still suffering from the wobbly "jello-legs" feeling and couldn't always tell whether what we were feeling was real or somatic in nature.

I was escorted to the *Eveque* (Bishop) of the Episcopal Diocese of Haiti) Monseigneur Bishop Jean Zaché Duracin.

"Mon Pere," I exclaimed.

He beamed at me.

"I heard of your efforts. Thank you for your good works!"

"How is your wife?"

"Injured, but alive" he responded.

"*Grace a Dieu*, and your house in Petion Ville?"

"It was not in Petion Ville, but Turgeau (near my apartment). It is completely flat. I couldn't even get inside to look around."

"*Desolée*, Monseigneur."

"You should rest the night here with us." I nodded.

"Monseigneur, have you any news of Jude Harmon, the American seminarian who was teaching here."

The crowd surrounding us parted, and there was Jude, my friend and fellow guest house occupant who had recently relocated to a dormitory at the Episcopal University the last trip I'd made to Haiti (was it only a month ago? Seemed like years, now)

"Manmi Jeanne!"

"Jude!"

We embraced, and he set about finding a place for me to stay. I helped set up a tent, but could not bear to sleep where I could not see the stars, so I made my bed on the bare ground a few feet away from the bishop's tent and cushioned my head on my gym bag.

Something poked my head, and I reached inside the bag and removed the Cross of the Risen Christ, which had been on the refectory wall of the guest house.

I arose and handed the Cross to the bishop, who accepted it with tears in his eyes and a tremor in his hands.

Return to Service

I returned to my spot and had only just lay down my head when the call came:

"Jeanne! *Medicin* (doctor) Jeanne!"

"*Oui, M'ap vini*"

I responded and gathered up my now largely depleted supplies.

Jude spoke: "Can you come? Michee was trapped at the school and they rescued her but she needs medical attention. There is supposed to be a doctor here who is a seminarian, but no one can find him at the moment. Can you come?"

"*M'ap vini*" I sighed and followed.

They brought me out of the campus and down the street a ways.

There, lying on a mattress on the sidewalk was a young woman. I later learned that she had been a 1st grade teacher at St. Trinite elementary school, who had been teaching a class at the college when the tremors hit. She became trapped under the building when it fell.

She appeared to be in her late 20's or early 30's, had very short hair, and was lying on her belly, with one hand reaching to grasp the upper end of the mattress.

I bent down and touched her cheek. She was ice-cold.

"She's in shock. We have to get her somewhere and use more blankets to warm her."

I gestured to see what was beneath the incredibly bloody curtain or tablecloth that covered her legs.

They gently rolled back the covering.

"Oh, no," I thought. The crushing injury...

I knew she would not, could not survive, but her friends and rescuers were so earnest, so loving, so hopeful, that I pretended we could make a difference.

I noted a huge, gaping, split wide-open wound on her upper thigh and more of the skin-shearing, burned looking patches that had become so familiar to me.

I disinfected, padded and tied a pressure bandage around her leg, but she'd lost so much blood already!

Then I walked behind the crew as they gently lifted her near-bier and carried her back to the campus of the College St. Pierre.

Once there, I blessed her and said the healing prayer over her. I made them get several covers for her, and told them to sit vigil: one person for each hour so that they would always be alert, and to come and get me immediately if her breathing changed.

I returned to my hard pallet of ground, brushed away a few more pieces of concrete, lay down with a spiraling motion to spare my knee and looked up at the sky.

It was a beautiful night with many stars, and as it had been during the previous night, also filled with many shooting stars.

Less than an hour later the call came:

"Manmi Jeanne!"

"M'ap vini"

I hurried to Michee's side.

"Manmi, you said to come if her breathing changed."

I bent down. Her breathing was still rapid, but more even

and perhaps a bit deeper. Not Cheynes-Stokes! Maybe there was hope.

I checked her pulse: high, but close to normal range.

Her temperature was close to normal again so that she was a little warm to the touch.

"She's doing okay for now" I said. "Call me again if there is any change."

I returned to the ground.

Perhaps 20 minutes later they called me again.

She was hemorrhaging from her nose, eyes and mouth. They were trying to stem the bleeding with a cloth.

I suspected a brain hemorrhage. Her breathing stopped. She gurgled.

I reached down to take her pulse at the carotid. It was very faint, very thready, so light and fast—like a butterfly's wings.

And then it was no more.

"Desolée" I said. "Elle est morte." (I'm sorry. She's dead.)

They rolled her body onto her back, and I gently closed a pair of eyes for the seventh time today. Time of death: 10 pm. Cause of death: massive and pervasive trauma.

I witnessed as they tried to close her mouth and cross her arms. I marveled at the tenderness with which they tied her two big toes together, then reverently covered her body with a sheet.

I turned and walked to a couple of young men standing nearby and begged a cigarette and smoked it. I am not a smoker, and have been asthmatic for many years, but that night I was shaking so badly that I needed the cigarette for medicinal purposes.

I returned to lie on the ground. Then, as if from outside of myself, observed my body enter shock:

I began to shake, I felt ice-cold, my teeth began to chatter. A man sitting in a chair near me handed me his shirt to try and warm me.

But this cold went soul-deep. No shirt, sweater or blanket would do the job.

"Tsunami!"

Suddenly three boys ran through the camp from the direction of the ruined school.

"*Dlo! Dlo! Dlo!*" they shouted as they ran.

"What is it?" I asked the Bishop.

"They are saying it is a tsunami coming" he replied.

"Well, sometimes that does happen after an earthquake" I answered.

The camp erupted as people fled the coming waters.

I strung my laptop across my shoulders, attached my gym bag to my rolling trumpet case, and followed the crowd. My fanny pack, with my apartment key for home in the States, my medical record card and cash had already disappeared.

Up, up and up we climbed through the debris-filled streets into Canape Vert.

Cars honked to part the crowds and people shoved and bumped their way past slower people like and including me.

I had almost reached the Comissarat (Police Station) of Canape Vert when I stopped, exhausted, removed my gym bag and laptop bag, lowered the handle of my trumpet case and sat down.

"Wait a minute" I thought. "A tsunami requires a large, deep source of water in which to build. Gonave Bay, north-west of Port-au-Prince is not that big or deep, and La Gonave Island is a big obstacle that is in the way. No tsunami could hit us here."

I turned and made my way back down the hill.

As I reached the Sacred Heart Hospital (now closed and fallen), I stopped again, beyond fatigue.

A man was standing there, smoking a cigarette. His son, a boy of perhaps 12 or 13 years of age, lay dead at his feet on the sidewalk in front of the hospital entrance.

"*Ici*" he said. "*Je t'aiderai*" (I will help you.)

He took my trumpet case and began rolling it down the hill.

"*Ki kote ou vle alé?*" (Where are you going?)

"*Le seminaire episcopale.*"(The Episcopal Seminary)

"*Li tombé.*" (It has fallen.)

"*Oui, mais le terrain sur le college Ste. Pierre a un camp. L'éveque est la.*" (Yes, but the field at the College Ste. Pierre has a camp. The Bishop is there.)

"*D'accord.*" (Okay.)

About halfway down the block he turned into a passageway.

"*Pou ki sa ou pasé la?*" (Why are you going there?)

"*Li pli kout.*" (It's shorter.)

I grew uneasy, and tried to follow him quickly, since I wasn't sure that he would not try to steal my trumpet or attack me in the darkness.

Because I was looking up, I didn't see the piece of iron gate lying across my path. I fell, hard, onto my hands and knees.

I collapsed into tears. "Oh, Jesus! Ow! Ow! Oh, my Jesus!"

My new friend returned to assist me up to my feet and hugged me until I stopped crying. We slowly returned to the slightly more lighted street to continue to the seminary.

My escort smelled of beer and, at first, when we got to the campsite, Pere Fin-Fin didn't want to let him stay in the camp.

But I explained how he had assisted me when I fell, and we soon returned to a spot covered by a plastic sheet to lie down.

The gentleman arranged my possessions into a sort of barricade around us and I sank down, exhausted and in pain. He put his arms around me, and I naively and gratefully thought he was going to try and comfort me.

Then I felt him grasping for my breasts.

"*Non*" I said, pushing him away. "*Gen moun.*" (No, there are people here.)

"*J'ai le bleu*" he insisted and placed my hand on his exposed genitals.

"*Non!*" I replied more firmly. "*Je suis soeur de Jesus! Ce n'est pas possible pour moi!*" (I am a sister of Jesus and it is not possible for me!)

I began to shake and cry and described the past day and a half in detail. He calmed and actually did then try to comfort me, but now the shock had returned and I was shivering violently and my teeth were chattering hard again.

Another person passed a thin fabric piece to me (probably a sheer curtain), to cover my short-sleeved arms from the really cold wind that was blowing.

I slept, fitfully, but I did finally sleep a bit.

Come morning, my escort kissed me chastely on the forehead and departed. I think I may have seen him, at a distance, later that morning, but we did not acknowledge each other.

Evacuation

Thursday morning word began to come of an evacuation of all American citizens. The embassy was arranging for military flights to remove American citizens immediately.

I resolved that I would not leave. I knew I still had much more work to do, since I had a range and variety of skills that could be applied at need.

My friend, Jude, was frantically searching for our friend Mallory, whom he had not seen since the tsunami scare the night before.

"I'm going to go home" he told me. "I came here to teach, and my school and students are no longer here, so I don't think there is anything else for me to do."

I hugged him, and wished him well. I later heard that he had successfully gotten out, as had Mallory.

I went to the Eveque, to report for my next project.

"Monseigneur, I need to return to Ste. Trinite. There are robes there that can be used as blankets against the cold, especially for the children." I was referring particularly to the handicapped children from St. Vincent's school, who were on the campus with us.

"N'est ce pas voiture" he replied (there is no car.)

"I can walk. It will take time, but we will have the robes tonight."

"Go, and God bless you." He marked the Sign of the Cross on my forehead.

My student, Carl-Henri, and his girlfriend accompanied me.

As we reached Michee's corpse, not yet collected by her family, I whispered a gentle requiem.

We reached Avenue Christophe and began to walk toward the Champ de Mars. I had traveled perhaps a block and a half when I heard someone call my name.

"Jeanne!" Miraculously, here was Fritz "Frito" Leroy, my bass-playing brother from Jacmel. Frito was here in Port-au-Prince with his girlfriend when the earthquake arrived.

He told me that Pierre, our brother, was in Jacmel for a funeral, and that they had spoken by cell phone and everyone at the Leroy home and the music school was okay (no deaths), but many of the students' homes had collapsed, and everyone was sleeping out of doors.

I hugged him and blessed him and asked him to give everyone my love and blessings and continued on my way.

I realized we were close to the OPC office (office of the protector of the citizens in Haiti), the workplace of my dear friend, Florence Elie. I knew that she often worked late hours and was concerned to know if she was okay. I decided we would make a brief detour to check on Florence and her staff.

We walked up the hill, past the devastated Sacred Heart Hospital to the corner where Sacred Heart church once stood. Now the church looked like it had been hit by a bomb, but the crucifix out front remained standing as a sad witness to all the destruction surrounding it.

Down the street, stepping around rubble and downed wires, we arrived at the street to the OPC. Florence's elderly uncle's house on the corner nearest Sacred Heart church was completely collapsed. Would her office still be standing? We moved up the street: I was confused: is it this yard? Or the next?

Finally we arrived to see the gates closed and padlocked. Looking through the keyhole, I could see no rubble on the ground, and the house was still standing!

Glory be to God! If she was here, she is okay.

I took out a pen (the very one with which I wrote the notes which began this book) and wrote on the gate:

> Manmi Flo:
>> I am alive. I am either @ Ste. Trinite or College Ste. Pierre. I send you my love and blessings.

I signed it with my signature and the trumpet with which I dot the "I" in my first name.

Carl-Henri noticed neighbors sitting outside their house next door and suggested we speak with them. It turned out that one of them was Marie-Josée, who had worked at US Aid with my good friend Marie-Claire Salomon (who now worked at the US embassy).

She told us that everyone left, whole, Tuesday evening from the OPC.

As she was speaking, another voice broke in:

"Madame Jeanne" I turned.

"Oui?"

"C'est Dominic."

Florence's chauffeur, who'd driven us to the apartment Tuesday afternoon before the quake!

He loaded my bags, Carl-Henri and his girlfriend, and me into the suv, and we started up the hill to Thomassin to get Flo. I planned to leave my things at Flo's where I knew they would be safe and continue back down to work at Ste. Trinite.

As we drove through Canape Vert, we had to re-route frequently. Many sections of road were blocked by collapsed buildings. Every school was down, and the smell of death was already apparent, hanging like a pall across the landscape, like the omnipresent dust cloud that stirred with the passage of the car, but did not break apart.

People walked with masks, handkerchiefs or even shirts drawn across their mouth and nose.

At school after school after school, frantic parents sought for a way to find their lost children...

As we climbed the hill, more and more destruction was revealed: honey-combed houses on the hillside collapsed like houses of cards or dominoes cascaded downwards. Yet strangely, mere meters away others still stood, seemingly unaffected.

Tall churches and multi-story buildings and buildings with thick, concrete-slab roofs seemed to be the worst-affected. Yet St. Pierre Catholic Church and St. James the Just Episcopal Church, both in Petion Ville, appeared to be untouched.

As we ascended the Kenscoff Road toward Thomassin, there was less and less visible damage, though everywhere there were weary pilgrims, trudging on the road, carrying all their worldly possessions on their heads or backs, their children in their arms.

Finally we reached the entrance to Florence's yard, but it was blocked by debris from a fallen retaining wall just uphill from the driveway. Domenic and his two helpers tried to move some of the stones, but eventually we left the car on the side of the road and walked up the long, leaf-strewn driveway.

It was cold here, as it often is in the mountains of Haiti, but the air was so clean and so fresh! Soon we topped the hill and saw Flo's house, nestled into the hillside: intact!

And there, face beaming with welcome was Manmi Flo herself, Florence Elie Protectrix du Citoyens et Citoyennes du l'Haïti!

I couldn't remember feeling so happy or relieved.

We entered and she offered us all coffee and told me to take a shower. (I was still covered with stone dust from the fall of the school). A shower sounded heavenly!

And she had a basket, filled with my clothing from a previous visit, so I have fresh, clean clothing to wear!

But first, the shower, during which I realized just how much debris had lodged in my hair and scalp. The water ran black, then gray, and then finally ran clear off me.

I gingerly explored my body to discover excruciatingly painful areas all up and down my right side, from my head to my ankles.

My feet, miraculously, seemed to be okay, especially lucky since I'd been wearing flip-flops during the tremblement.

I walked out into the living room in socks, underpants and a sleeveless t-shirt to winces all around as everyone saw my bruised arm and legs.

"Here" said Flo. "Why don't you lie down on the couch for a bit?"

This was around 4:30 pm, since it took us several hours to ascend the mountain.

I did so, and I did not awaken again until after 6 am the next (Friday) morning.

When I awakened, everything hurt and I was disoriented.

Then everything came back to me at once, and I started to shake and to weep.

First Friday

Florence had covered me with a doubled sheet to warm me and protect me from the mosquitoes. I rose, with difficulty and donned my clothing (some tan chinos and an OPST polo shirt over my sleeveless t-shirt).

Flo told me to eat, but I could not yet. I sipped gingerly at water and decided I will take my meds and vitamins every other day so they will last longer.

Dominic was due to arrive and we decided I would go back down the mountain with him (he had taken Carl-Henri and his girlfriend back down on Thursday evening while I slept.)

We set goals for the trip:

1. Pick up Flo's friend, Michelle, and her mother and son.
2. Take me to College Ste. Pierre, then to Ste. Trinite to get more of my things, including clothing and meds.
3. Stop by OPC to evaluate and get some face masks from Flo's desk.

As we traveled back down the hill, "Do-Do" (Dominic's nickname) pointed out various horrors to me and advised me when to cover my mouth and nose against the dust and the smell of death.

When we stopped at Michelle's, the neighbors told us her house *"tombé"* (fell down) and she was not there.

We left and headed over to College St. Pierre, where I needed to see the Eveque. First, though, I spoke with Sister Marjorie, of the Sisters of St. Margaret who told me that my American friends, Jude and Mallory, who taught at the seminary have decided to be evacuated with other Americans.

"I cannot leave" I told her. "My place is here. *J'ai beaucoup de travail ici.*" (I have lots of work to do here).

"That's natural" she replied. "I would expect nothing less. Your connection with these children is more pastoral in nature."

I marveled. I had told no one in Haiti about my thoughts about ministry, other than that I considered myself to be a missionary and here this 86 year old sister saw me clearly.

"Manmi Jeanne?" I turned to see Lalanne, another of my music students.

"I am a busker now, helping to collect bodies, but I wanted to greet you!"

I blessed him and asked angels to guard him then turned to seek the Bishop.

I apologized for my absence and explained my injuries and collapse, but then told him that I had a car at my disposal, courtesy of Florence Elie. I said that we would return to Ste. Trinite to get the robes we had not achieved the day before.

"Please give me your blessing" I asked.

He marked the Sign of the Cross on my forehead:

"May God bless you, now and always."

I turned to go.

We drove to Ste. Trinite and found the gates chained and locked.

But wait: the pedestrian gate was just wrapped with chains, not locked.

Dodo opened it and I entered, calling for Edward.

He appeared, and then called for Raphael, who went searching for the keys. Soon he returned: the person with the keys had gone to the Champ de Mars.

How could we get inside?

Edward climbed up, over the wall and opened the parents' gate to the sidewalk from the inside. We walked in.

Operation Salvage, Part II

The men were insecure about entering the building, but I sent them into one of the classrooms. We would make a chain, passing the robes from person to person, bit by bit.

Edward waited at the bottom, in the courtyard below the guest house to catch the robes I threw down to him.

I climbed again up into the guest house.

The smell of death was much stronger here, with the ruins of the professional school so close. I don't think I will ever be able to tolerate the smell of teriyaki beef or beef jerky again, because that was very much the sort of smell, although it was far, far more pervasive.

And that horrible, cloyingl, sick-sweet smell was all over the city. The government said that they estimated 200,000 to 300,000 people were dead, but those of us who traveled into the city to work or do rescue operations all believe the numbers to be more like 1.2 or 1.3 MILLION people who had lost their lives in the earthquake.

Some probably survived for a day or two after the quake, some re-entered buildings after the initial quake, only to be lost in a strong aftershock. Many died immediately, and as Sister Marjorie said "Flew straight to heaven."

I entered my room to see that my student had begun to fill a box with robes, but never finished.

I turned and emptied the dresser in the wall of robes and supplies, then turned to the closet, which was filled with robes and surplices.

I realized that I must remove every hanger, or risk injuring my helper waiting down below the balcony. That extended the time it took to gather the robes a bit, but finally I had the box filled to overflowing and dragged it out to the edge of the balcony.

I began to toss armfuls over the railing. As each fell, it was collected and relayed to the men waiting in the classroom. Once all the robes were collected in the classroom, we would bring them out to the waiting truck, and thence to College St. Pierre.

I took the tablecloth off the refectory table, too. And then I thought of the other guest room. It was locked, but I thought I could break in through the window in the door.

As it turned out, that was an incredibly easy thing to do, and I understood why the gate downstairs had always been kept double-locked.

Within this room I found more sheets and pillows, shirts and t-shirts but no more robes. I soon tossed all of these down.

I used the toilet, considered trying to break the lock on the pantry door, but left that for another day.

I stopped, once last time, to listen for any rapping. It had been three days—were they still alive, my rappers?

"*Allo?*" I called. "*Allo?*" ("hello?")

Nothing…nothing at all.

I wept, briefly, then made a large Sign of the Cross and whispered a requiem prayer.

Then went back down the stairs and relocked the gate.

We returned to College Ste. Pierre with the robes and solicited help with the unloading.

"Manmi Jeanne, that man in the truck across the street wants to talk to you."

"Who is it?"

"I don't know."

A man in a yellow hard-hat approached me.

"Jeanne!"

"Dickins! Thanks Be to God! Are you okay?"

"*Oui, ca va.*" ("Yes, I'm okay")

Dickins Princivil is a talented musician: cellist, bassist, and composer. I had conducted the world premiere of the orchestral/choral edition of his powerful piece "Transitions" on the Ste. Cecile concert in memory of Hughes Leroy on 21 November, 2009.

He, his wife, their children and their house were all fine—another miracle!

I returned to the Bishop.

"Monseigneur, I must leave for a brief while."

"You will leave through the Dominican Republic?"

"No, mon pere. I am not leaving my Haiti when she needs me! I will be going back to Thomassin for a few days to recover from my injuries and then I will return back here, to work."

"Thank-you for all your good work."

"You will distribute the robes?"

"We will store them safely."

"No, Monseigneur, they are for God's people who need them now. We will obtain replacements if needed when the time comes, I assure you!"

"We will keep them safe and distribute them only to the neediest."

I hesitated, reluctant to relinquish control, the old alpha personality struggling against my new found life of service.

"I know I can trust you. You are a man of God as I am a woman of God! May I please have your blessing?"

This time, the blessing was substantial, including prayers for my healing and strength.

"I will be back in a few days"

I promised, and returned to the truck.

We returned to Michelle's, coming in from the other end of the street. As we approached, a low-hanging wire caught on the spotlight above the windshield of the truck.

We backed up a bit, and I lifted the wire (marveling that I was not afraid to do so with bare hands!) so we could pass.

This time, friends of Michelle's loaded several large containers of her belongings into the truck.

"Where are Michelle and her family?" I asked, in French.

"Not here" was the response, and we continued over to the OPC.

Hurry Up (and wait!)

The gate to the OPC was locked; the guardian was missing in action.

From Marie Josée next door we learned that he had gone to assist in taking a dead body back to a family in Tabarre, but would be back in a couple of hours.

We sat down to wait. I spoke with Marie Josée and we exchanged contact information. We talked about *Instrumental Change, Inc (ICI)*, my non-profit charitable corporation; and about US Aid. I learned from Marie Josée that Marie Claire had lent her car to Pierre for him to attend the funeral of a friend in Jacmel, so he was there when the earthquake arrived.

Reports from Jacmel were not good: the whole downtown area was said to be flattened: "There is no more 'Jacmel'" people said.

Inside my heart, I quietly wept. I loved Jacmel: its easy feeling, its love of Kanaval, its many beaches and galleries, and, of course, my beloved Ecôle de Musique Dessaix Baptiste.

I wondered and worried about my family-friends, colleagues and students. It was in Jacmel that I first cemented my covenant with Haïti. Would I ever see it again?

Marie Josée invited me to sit with her family and introduced me, explaining how she had seen me perform at Ste. Trinite many times.

I met her nephew, a pianist and producer. We talked about collaborating in the future.

Then I met her 18 year old niece, Stefanie, who calls herself a "survivor". She haltingly told me of the loss of her best friend, Kiki, who had gone to visit another friend. The house they were in collapsed on top of them, killing them both instantly. Stefanie regretted not being with them.

"What do I have for a future? No school, no job—nothing" she cried.

I consoled and blessed her.

She told of being at school at St. Rose of Lima.

"I saw from the road that it seems to be still standing" I commented.

"Yes" she said. "Most of it is, but I was in the chapel and had to run across tables to the door. There were five others behind me, but when I got out none of them were there. I went back and opened the door again and all I could see was dust upon dust. No people...I don't know if any of them survived."

She told of her Mom, an anesthesiologist, who was working at the hospital when the earthquake happened.

I knew this probably meant her Mom was dead, buried under the rubble, but I didn't deny her some small hope.

"Where were you when it happened?" she asked me.

So I told her of La Salle Ste. Cecile, of the kids with me, of rescuing the two students and finding Madame Lahens' body, of the route out of the collapsed school, of the trips back into the guest house, and of the clinic, and the deaths and the miracles, and of my ultimate collapse...

"Just a minute" she said.

She went into her house and returned with a can of vitamin milk and a packet of water.

"Drink these" she said. "It's not much, but you've been through so much..."

I thanked her and I drank. We exchanged emails (I had no cell phone number to give her, as mine had been lost in the ruins) and promised to stay in touch as best as possible.

Finally the guardian for the OPC arrived with the keys, and we entered the gate and the front courtyard of the OPC.

The building still stood with remarkably little rubble outside.

But upon entering the building, I discovered that there were multiple, large cracks inside on many of the walls, although the walls were still standing.

I made my way gingerly up the stairs, through tumbled rubble on the staircase, and into Flo's office.

Her computer monitor had fallen, and there was dust everywhere, but remarkably little other damage.

I reset the monitor on its stand, found the box of face masks Flo had asked us to get, and looked quickly around to see what else she might need.

I considered her calendar book—no. Then I saw the copy of my book, "Trumpeting By Nature" which I had given her on Tuesday, sitting on her desk.

I grabbed the book, thinking it would provide reading material, and exited the office, being careful to relock everything.

At the foot of the stairs I found the kitchen and went into it, seeking something to drink. In the little refrigerator I found a bottle of Coke and a bottle of Sprite. I took them: gave the Coke to Do-Do, who still had much driving to do, and took the Sprite for myself.

We hopped into the truck and started back up the hill. By now it was 7:30 pm and very, very dark.

We stopped in Petion Ville, near St. Pierre's Catholic Church, which was remarkably intact, to retrieve something from a vendor, then continued up the mountain side.

It was about 9 pm when we finally arrived back at Florence's house and I handed the box of masks and the book to her.

"How did you know to get the book" she exclaimed. "I was looking everywhere for it."

I shrugged and turned to go to bed, satisfied with having completed two missions today. I slept.

Personal Injuries

First and foremost: PTSD. Any large rumble (even wind or airplanes flying over head) sets my pulse racing and the fight-or-flight syndrome into deep action.

2nd: Serious, deep contusion of the outside of my right upper arm.

3rd: Asthma does not appear to be an issue. I am breathing well, occasionally coughing mildly from the dust, but no wheezing and no tightness in my chest.

4th: Major tenderness on my right side, from just below the ribcage up to about the third rib.

5th: Right ileac crest is severely bruised and sore, as is right buttocks, which is sore and cramping a lot.

6th: Right knee and lower leg very bruised and sore.

7th: Left knee and shin very bruised and sore

8th: Both palms are abraded, with some puncture wounds (three) on right palm.

9th. A road burn sort of contusion on upper, outer right forearm

10th: Both shoulders and elbows feel effects of fall on Wednesday night.

11. Am eating very little, 1 or 2 times per day, 4 oz. or less.

12. Am being very cautious with fluids about 16 oz./day.

13. Am taking meds and vitamins every other day to try to make them last, since I don't know how long it will be before I can get more of them.

14. Sadness is at times overwhelming, but prayer is helping me to cope.

Contact!

Friday evening, before I went to sleep, Florence tried to call Laënnec Hurbon for me. Repeatedly we dialed and dialed and dialed, trying to get through the lines.

Finally: "Allo?" a familiar, beloved voice.

"Laënnec?"

"Oui, c'est Laënnec."

"C'est Jeanny"

"Oh, Jeanny! Comment vas-tu?"

"I'm alive, and grateful to God that you are, too!"

"Where are you now?"

"I'm at Florence's house."

"Let me talk to Florence."

I passed the phone. Flo and Laënnec talked for several more minutes and then, when he felt he couldn't talk any more, the call ended.

On Saturday, we spoke again, and I learned that he had, indeed, been coming to jazz band, and was on the Champs des Mars, just outside the palace when the quake hit. He saw the palace fall right in front of him.

Then he turned his car around and headed back up, into Canape Vert, to try to go home.

Because so many of the streets were blocked by fallen buildings, he had left his car somewhere on the street in Canape Vert and made his way, on foot, back to his home in Bel Vil.

He arrived at 10 pm to find his house intact and his sister and Canadian house guests safe.

"Mai, Jeanny" he said sadly, "*J'ai perdu beaucoups des eleves et des colleagues et amis.*" (I have lost many students, colleagues and friends)

Quisqueya University, for which Laënnec had been a co-founder, had built a beautiful and modern new campus on the hill in Turgeau.

There were many newly-entering students at the campus, taking an entrance exam and due to attend a reception following the exam with most of the professors of the school.

All perished when the entire new campus collapsed into dust during the earthquake.

Had Laënnec not been coming to rehearsal with me, he likely would have perished also.

He was searching for a way to get to Paris where he could be a spokesman to the world about Haiti, and secure more aid for her.

"I will call you again" he said, in English.

"Big hugs and I love you!" I replied.

"Okay, bisous!" He hung up.

Saturday, 16 January

Saturday morning we discussed food, water, gas, and logistics. Flo, her daughter Guisou and I split one power bar for breakfast.

I sat down and began to write of my experiences, and the words would not stop. Hour after hour after hour, this story poured from me.

At dinner time, I had 4 ounces of bread with some sloppy joe mix on it. Because the bread was a little moldy, I had some Barbancourt (Haitian rum) mixed with lime juice as I ate.

A neighbor's son, Enoch, arrived to speak with Flo. I noted his lovely speaking voice and told him he should sing. He looked at me as if to say "Why bother?" but I will continue to encourage him to reconsider.

Florence is a powerhouse of strength: she plans the food, the use of water for drinking, toilet, washing.

She has brought her elderly, infirm mother and her sister to her brother Fred's house next door. Her younger brother, Philippe, who is a gifted photographer and his girlfriend, Pasqual, are camping on the grounds in a tent.

FLO's QUAKE EXPERIENCE

Florence described her own experience during the *"tremble-ment du terre."* (earthquake, literally "trembling of the earth")

"I was on the road, between the two airports (in Tabarre). The road began to pitch and heave the car about as if it were a match-stick on a violent ocean!"

It is from Flo that I learned that there had been 2 quaking motions occurring simultaneously: one moved from side-to-side, the other came straight up. The two motions balanced each other somewhat, or else much of Centerville might have fallen into a huge crevasse.

The epicenter was said to be at or near the national palace. (Later we learned it was about 10 kilometers west of the city, heading to Leogane).

It registered 7.3 on the Richter scale. The actual quake was said to have lasted 17 seconds, (later we learned it was 31 seconds, then finally 43 seconds long) but in the thoughts, dreams and experiences of those of us who lived through it, it will never be over, I think.

Every rumble, every vibration sees us gasping, reaching for one another, racing to door frames or outside, trembling so much ourselves that we cannot really discern if the earth is actually still moving or not.

And every time I close my eyes, I hear that lost, anonymous student in the professional school: "Tap...Tap...Tap-tap-Tap..."ing his farewell to the world...

Sunday Piecemeal Memories

During the earthquake, the stage of the Salle St. Cecile tilted up at the downstage edge and slanted downwards toward the back wall and the right-hand wall (toward Avenue Mgr. Guilloux and Rue des Miracles), causing the piano to roll backwards and toward the right.

The piano bench, at which I had been seated, was displaced by a large piece of concrete (perhaps from the stage left balcony), the dimensions of which were about 6 feet long, by 15 inches or so square.

Just in front of the edge of the stage, stage left, in the orchestra pit, a volcano-like eruption that was about 30 to 40 inches high rose from the floor.

All areas I have seen that had had the kind of concrete, decorative blocks with holes in them collapsed.

Solid concrete staircases (such as from the main lobby of the auditorium up to the penthouse offices, and the stairs to the guest house) remained intact, as did walls reinforced by metal, gate-like sections (but not those sections containing steel bars or cables, all of which appear to have fallen).

The dome-like sections of the ceiling at the stage end of the Salle St. Cecile remained largely intact, in and of themselves, but entire spans of them (from left to right) fell to the stage level.

It was one of these bell-like sections that preserved the lives of me and my student, David Saintilus. Another protected the trumpeters at the base of the stage.

My water bottle, cell phone and calendar book, which were all on the piano desk, all disappeared into the rubble at the rear of the stage.

Oddly, I did not drop all the music sheets in my hand, and my laptop bag (sans laptop, which I had left in the guest house to make the bag lighter) was on the same chair, in the same exact spot, untouched by the block that would have killed me.

The metal doorframe from the first level of the auditorium to the Studio 24/Percussion studio hallway (to which we fled between aftershocks) was somewhat twisted and skewed at about a 30 degree angle from true, but it did stay in place, as did the stage-left upstage metal doors.

The large, ascending levels of the auditorium also seemed largely intact, thought the penthouse office suite and classrooms on either side collapsed, as did the stage- right balcony.

The stage-left balcony held, which is probably why we were able to exit through the damaged corridor beneath it.

My godson's bass was buried beneath debris, I don't know if it could have been salvaged (later it was salvaged)—my concern at that point was getting the kids out.

The stage-left corridor's roof was down, but was mostly metal supports and acoustic tile sections. That was mixed on the floor with debris from the walls of the corridor.

Remy Jean's scalp was lacerated by one of the metal pieces from the ceiling.

Ariane did not know where her children were (younger students)— they usually did homework in the Salle Ste. Cecile or the lunchroom/ antechamber while she taught and/or rehearsed. They had not been in the Salle Ste. Cecile and the antechamber had collapsed into the ruins of the professional school.

The piece of concrete from under which we rescued the little violinist and pulled the body of Madame Lahens, was at least five feet wide, ten inches thick and seven feet long/deep.

I honestly don't understand how even five of us were able to budge it, but once it was up, three of us were able to keep it up to get Madame Lahens' body out.

The little girl's violin and bow (and, ominously, a second bow) were left in the rubble.

Miraculously, the offices of Manmi Rose and Nicole St. Victor, as well as that of Guerlain and Pierre Leroy, and the original practice rooms remained intact, as did the Romel room beyond, though it had dropped some 10 or 12 feet down.

I did not examine the new practice room area (that came later), but I understand that is the area from which Skendre rescued Mannie Mejeun from under a fallen column (in the Hughes Leroy room, perhaps?)

The first room as you entered the EMST (Ecole de Musique Ste Trinite), which had a small stage and was used as a rehearsal hall for EIV(Ensemble Instrumental du Vents, or Wind Ensemble/Band) and mini-harmonie bands, was completely gone: the Romel room above it had crushed it completely. In fact, the wooden door that had been the entry from the elementary school was that which had been used as a slide from the window of the Romel room to the outside.

The portrait of the late Hector Lominy, first director of the OPST, which hung at the top of the stairs outside Manmi Rose's office, was broken beyond reprieve in the collapsed stairwell.

I think part of the structural issue was the lack of supporting columns and walls in the honeycomb of classrooms, offices and hallways in the professional school beneath the music school.

The old auditorium, right of the elementary school playground, remained intact, though some walls were cracked. The area in front of the stage and the balcony above it and the first stairwell, next to the guest house passageway all remained largely intact, at least after the first earthquake.

Beside stage-right of the Salle Ste. Cecile, there was a stairway that led down, into the professional school. (There was a window right next to it, through which you could look down into a classroom).

The professional school was a maze/warren of rooms with the auto/machine/carpentry shops on the ground floor, the electrical and business/computer schools on the 2nd and 3rd floors.

I remember going down into the school with Pere David to print some music and talking to one of the teachers in the school about playing the violin again. He proudly told me in November that he was doing so.

And now he is gone...

GUEST HOUSE ODDITIES

My room and the other room on the second floor of the guest house were basically intact. My dresser had shifted approximately 30 degrees, and everything atop it and the other set of drawers had fallen to the floor (as had my trumpet, off its stand).

My laptop, in its protective sleeve, was dusty, but undamaged. My trumpet case was perfectly intact (Dillon's Music should use this for an ad), and I wish I had put my main trumpet inside of it before going to rehearsal so that it hadn't received the damage that made it unplayable for me.

In the refectory, the TV had tipped onto the table, but was undamaged. I tipped it back onto its stand to salvage the tablecloth for a blanket for College Ste. Pierre.

The bookshelves themselves in the refectory had not fallen, even the two on the left as you entered the dining room, which were just boards on brackets.

The kitchen was completely destroyed, and the sink/stove area clocked. Had Marlene been there, she would not have survived.

Tuesday, 19 January

On Monday night, I was told, it rained. While this was a blessing for those of us in the hills, I could only imagine the panic in the city.

Haitians fear rain. They believe they will become ill if they get soaked by rain. This fear seems to affect <u>all</u> Haitians, even my friends who are intellectuals.

The other issue, of course, was that the rain would wash pathogens out of the ruined buildings, actually spreading disease from the decaying corpses within. Also, I feared that the rain would add weight, solidifying the crumbled mortar and perhaps causing even more of the compromised structures to fall.

Today, Florence, as a minister-level official, would meet with the head of the Swiss International Red Cross. She was going to present my offer of service to them, based on my knowledge and experience, particularly since the quake.

I believed I had recuperated sufficiently to be of service again. Although the bruise on my right arm was still very tender, other areas seemed okay. I could lift, bend, and use my legs, feet and hands. And I could do more than simply pray—though my prayers were constant: I had begun, again, to say a complete Rosary (all three mysteries) each day.

I was also studying French, aided by my small dictionary and Florence's large dictionary.

I was also continuing to investigate and discern more specifics about my calling here in Haiti. I studied the writings of St. Theresa (Mother Theresa) of Calcutta. (To me there could be no question of her sainthood!) Much of what she has written resonates deeply within me, in particular her efforts to identify with the suffering of Christ, crucified.

This idea was first introduced to me through the literature of the Foculare movement by my Italian "Mama" Valentina Russolillo. Valentina had been a great support to me throughout my discernment process, and I could literally feel her prayers supporting me throughout the weeks following the earthquake.

I believed the idea of working for the Red Cross to be a good one and prayed that it was God's Will that they accept my service.

I would ask to be assigned to the Delmas 30's area, in the hope I might find news of Gaguy and my students there, or perhaps to Cite Soleil.

In this way, in this service, I might do hands-on healing, in the apostolic sense, as well as simple first aid as required, thus bringing Christ's Holy Presence, through my service, humbly, to God's people that they may know peace and healing.

I knew that the earthquake was not God's doing, but a consequence of humanity's rape of the Earth. Had we not disturbed the subterranean stores of fossil fuels that provided a smooth surface and cushion upon which the tectonic plates could move, we would not be subject to such terrifying displays of the earth's damaging power.

I do believe that it is God's Will for those of us who do believe and have survived this cataclysm, to minister tenderly, gently and peacefully to God's flock. As sheep who will panic and scatter at a cross word, so are God's humble people, who require the Gentle Shepherd in their midst if they are to feel safe and sound.

Such a person is Bishop Jean Zaché Duracin, who slept on the ground with all of the rest of us on the soccer field at College St. Pierre for week after week after week. This wise, gentle and humble man is a true figure of Christ among us, and I am honored to be able to say that I have served under his guidance!

Wednesday, 20 January

We awoke to a minor quake at about 6:15 am this morning. All of us jumped from bed and headed for the outside. But it didn't do more than shake our beds, the house and the dishes (like quakes I've felt in New England). It only lasted about 5 seconds, but it was enough to make us all question our "imaginary" tremors that we've all been feeling for the past week. Later we learned it had been a 6.1 magnitude quake centered near Ste. Marc.

It has left us all with the "jello" feeling again, though. Your body becomes confused: sounds become sensations. The sound of a big plane flying overhead: could it be another quake? Then the pitch changes and you know it's just another plane.

But still, you feel all those vibrations viscerally. You have trouble shutting off those extraneous outer stimuli that we have mostly learned to ignore in this busy modern world we think we know so well.

And then the real world awakens and shakes us thoroughly, to our core and hers!

We are all hyper-acute, hypersensitive: prophetic dreams and premonitions abound. This whole experience seems to have awakened primal urges, tendencies and awareness.

11 am: We have just heard that the tremors/minor quake we experienced here at 6 am this morning struck St. Marc with a major quake of 6.0 – 6.3 on the Richter scale.

This is very disturbing, because St. Marc is on a separate fault line from that of the Leogane/Port-au-Prince/Jacmel fault line through Delmas and Petion Ville.

If we are dealing with two major fault lines, the evidence does not bode well for the *ouest*(west) department of Haïti (or the *Sud-Est*(south-east), either, since the first fault runs to there).

Early this morning there was a heavy fog over us. Then it cleared for a couple of hours, now it is back again, heavier than ever.

It is as if the rest of the world has disappeared behind this veil of fog: we hear the airplanes coming and going, but cannot see them. Speaking of airplanes: commercial flights were to have resumed today, then the date was pushed back to January 25th. Now they are saying "within ten days of January 25th."

I am hoping to be able to make an international call soon to Marty Rooney, my trumpet-playing lawyer, so he can talk to the band members for his upcoming wedding reception on February 12th.

It's not looking like I will be able to get back there for the wedding at this stage. I feel bad about that, since Marty has done so much for me and for ICInc, but there really isn't much that I can do about it at this point. Even the "mass evacuation of American citizens" appears to have been a myth, or at the very least a gross exaggeration.

We know that the US Marines have begun to arrive. That is a verified fact, and a comfort, but beyond that…nothing.

Even the Swiss Red Cross director only made a tour of the affected areas and left right away again.

That this event should have struck the poorest nation in this hemisphere is both ironic and a bit of a blessing:

It is a blessing because we who are here in Haiti are already accustomed to having so little on which to subsist.

It is ironic, because even that little is sorely tried by this tragedy, as are the hearts, bodies, minds and spirits of the precious Haitian people.

It is also ironic that this should have occurred during pre-Kanaval time, when the populace normally begins to escalate into the mad frenzy that characterizes Kanaval in Haiti.

Instead of Kanaval this is now a period of deep mourning: funerals instead of parades; faces masked by mourning instead of colorful papier maché.

Baron Samedi, the vaudoun lwa of death and the cemetery is surely dancing over the massed graves and unexcavated, collapsed ruins of Port-au-Prince, Delmas, Petion Ville, Bourdonville, Canape Vert, Jacmel, and now St. Marc.

I wished for the world to know and love my beloved Haiti… now it appears there are only tears.

Will we ever again see those bright, brilliantly white, welcoming smiles again?

Will Centerville ever again resound with that vibrant daily cacophony of music, traffic and business?

Will lovely Haiti, the pearl of the Caribbean, once again rise from death, disaster and destruction to dance and shine as the Belle of the Caribbean?

I can only pray and hope…

James 5:15

"And the prayer of faith shall save the sick, and the Lord shall raise him up; and if he has committed sins, they shall be forgiven him."

EVENING VISITORS

Florence returned home with two American doctors, from Oakland, California: Ramona (a surgeon) and Harold (an internist).

Ramona examined my arm, performed some diagnostic tests and told me I had soft tissue damage.

Then we sat down on the deck and began to talk… and talk. Everything flew out of me to these wonderful Christian doctors (who are also each ordained American Baptist ministers and have served in prisons and other 3rd world countries).

As I described the injuries and my attempts to provide first aid, they nodded and affirmed what I had done. They asked me to describe the injuries (not to worry about technical terminology, just describe, in detail, and they would fill in the rest of the information).

They asked so many questions, and I remembered details I'd forgotten (like the weird ear-popping sensation I'd felt just before the quake).

They explained about PTSD (some of which I had known before) and that the reason the victims with substantial lower body crushing died is that their damaged muscles sent out large amounts of enzymes that were toxic to the body. These were in such quantity that it overwhelmed the body's resources, causing kidney failure (hence the massive, general swelling and shut-down in urine output that I'd seen, but not understood).

Then Ramona rose, came over and dubbed me "Mammy Luke" (for St. Luke, the physician) and said they were naming me an honorary physician.

We joined hands and she prayed, blessing us and praising God for bringing us together and asking Him to guide, protect, strengthen and sustain us now and always and lead us to seek and do His will, in Jesus' Name. Amen.

Such power. Such grace. I felt so humbled and yet so uplifted. Ramona then went inside to talk to the others and Harold and I stayed outside, talking longer.

I told him of the anonymous "frapping" from the ruins of the professional school; how I had said "M'ap vini" (I'm coming) but had been unable to complete that pledge; how the knocking had ceased when I returned on Friday... and how this haunted me, even though I had prayed for the frapper(s).

Harold was wise. He told me that it was not <u>my</u> will that mattered, it was God's Will. And that we had attempted rescue, but since it was God's Will to call these souls home to Him, I must not focus on this any longer, but once again accept God's Will completely and submit to it.

He said to continue to pray and that God will compel me into the next phase of my calling, whatever and wherever that might be.

Later in the evening, when we were all bedded down for the night, we discussed Haitian society, politics and vaudou. I lent Rene's book by Alfred Metraux on vaudou to Ramona so she could grasp an overview of it.

I made a grand faux pas in disagreeing about the historical basis of a comment Guisou made about vaudou and Catholicism and Ramona rightfully chastised me. Somehow this opened a floodgate for Guisou and she spoke a lot about hers and her schoolmates' ideas about changing Haiti for the better.

If brilliant young people, such as Guisou Malary, can marshal their strengths and ideas, then Haiti indeed has a bright and fortunate future!

As we all began to drift into sleep, there was good natured jibing between Ramona and Harold about who would be snoring during the night.

Truth to tell, I think every one of us except Flo's little niece, Thais, did a bit of snoring, but we all slept.

Thursday, 21 January

I awoke about 1:15 am to some minor tremors(pictures shaking on the walls, and deep timpani rolls in the earth), but after prayer drifted back to sleep until 6 am when everyone rose as Flo needed to bring the doctors to a rendezvous with the other doctors they'd be joining today in the field.

Ramona and I spoke some more. She said distance study was fine for ministers and told me to go to seminary if I felt I really needed the "affirmation" otherwise she felt my calling was "to do, not to talk or intellectualize." We parted with a prayer and a blessing.

Two more serious tremors within 15 minutes of each other, beginning at 11:50 am.

2:05 pm Another serious tremor.

4:30 pm Ramona allowed me to use her US cell phone (a Blackberry) to call Der Hayr Vasken Kouzouian, my pastor.

I spoke with him, then with my dear friend, Karine Bagdasarian, a brilliant pianist who serves as organist at our church.

I then gave him phone numbers for my mother and my lawyer, and Florence's number to give to them. I also asked him to tell

Marty I probably would not be able to be back for Marty's Valentine's weekend wedding.

Then Florence had me come along as she led Harold and Ramona to the National Hospital, where they will work a 12 hour shift tonight, then return to the Dominican Republic for two days to collect their belongings, and then return to Haiti for more service. They are such blessings!

It appears that much more has fallen in Port-au-Prince since I left. The flag on the Champs des Mars is flying at half-mast.

But the USMC is here, thank God. I shouted *"Semper Fi!"* to some of the Marines on the sidewalk and they grinned back at me.

Then Flo passed me the phone. It was Marie Claire Salomon. "Pierre and all the family in Jacmel are fine" she told me.

"Gaguy is fine: one of his gates fell, but his house is completely intact."

Praise God for his mercy.

Marie Claire told me that Jim Watras, my friend and former colleague at the Waring School in Beverly, MA, who had come to Haiti with me in October of 2009, had called to ask about me, and that Vitalem Alriche and Janet and others have been asking about me.

She asked when I will leave and I told her I'm not leaving. As I told Der Hayr: "I have fully accepted the mantle of my ministry now and don't know when I will be back in the States, but please give my love and blessings to all!"

Friday, 22 January

I returned to the Ville with Florence today. She brought me to Ste. Trinite, where I went into the guest house and rescued Janet Anthony's string music, but was unsuccessful in finding my other medicine box. I will try to reach Remy today and hope that he has it in his possession. I would be staying at the refugee camp on the soccer field of the College Ste Pierre from now on.

While I was at Ste. Trinite, Gaguy Depestre came looking for me. It was a blessing to see and speak with him. He told me the wall between his house and the neighbor's house had "blown up" (collapsed) completely for more than 100 feet of its length, but that his house is intact.

Then he asked "Why us? Why Haïti?"

I told him there is no "why," it just <u>happened</u>. If there is any reason at all, it is the response of the earth to being raped of her fossil fuels for so long. And Haiti, being so close to Texas, received the brunt of it.

After Gaguy left, I walked to the palace to inquire again about Rico Jean, my conducting student. The entire old palace, where the band lived and worked, had collapsed. Many band members had perished.

But Rico is alive. And well, and uninjured.

His house, which was in Delmas, is destroyed, but his little concrete barracks survived. He plans to come and get me Sunday morning to go to Turgeau to assess the apartment.

Saturday, 23 January

I spoke with Florence this morning, and she will bring me my laptop and power cords later today. I will ask her then if the banks are open yet so that I can get some more money out and change what I have for smaller bills.

I spoke with Pierre Wilmique (the seminarian/doctor) early this morning as I was saying my prayers. He asked if I had a stethoscope and when I said I did not, promised to get another one for me.

I have seen a few of the children I treated at Ste. Trinite and they look good: wounds have closed and are healing, without infection. Praise God!

One of the girls with a broken leg was able to get a cast put on it, too. Another blessing.

I toured some of the fallen College Ste. Pierre: the top floor is nearly intact, the next floor down almost crushed completely, the ground floor is completely ground to powder. There is no way anyone could have survived in the lower two floors.

Lalanne told me of one student from the Professional School at Ste. Trinite who stayed in touch via his cell phone for 3 days until his battery (or he or both) died.

It is so difficult to think of him, in the ruins, hoping for rescue, receiving none. I pray his passing was easy and painless. I know he rests with the Lord, as do all the victims of these two horrible earthquakes.

May he rest in Peace and in eternal Light.

Today, in the afternoon, I met a surgeon from New Canaan, Connecticut, my home state. Dr. David Reed practices in Stamford. We spoke of my patients and discussed the injuries that I'd seen.

He served for a time in Hayasdan, in Armenia, after their earthquake. He told me that the stripping of flesh from the legs is called a "stocking injury" and the same thing on the arms/hands is called "degloving."

When I said I had, at first, thought I was seeing burns, he said these injuries are just like burns, in that both remove serious quantities of the skin and compromise the body's immune system.

I shared my procurement list with him and he said it was good. He also confirmed my concern that many here in Haiti must undergo amputations due to the extent of their injuries. I told him that Haiti is not a kind place for amputees. He said "The third world never is."

I was invited to have dinner with the Eveque and Sisters Mary Margaret and Therese. We discussed further salvage efforts at Ste. Trinite, beginning today.

Pierre Richard Etienne came to see me and told me he was able to get into the school through the Romel room and save his trumpet and his sister's violin.

I will try to get more instruments out if possible. Lalanne will help, Remy and Carl-Henri, perhaps, too.

I think EMST takes precedence over Turgeau for now. God is guiding me.

I spoke with Monseigneur after dinner about my experiences (including the miracle of the crazy man being struck dumb when I prayed to Jesus to do so), and asked if he thought I was crazy. He said "No" and smiled.

What a wonderful, kind and insightful leader this man is! I will willingly serve God with this man's guidance as long as I live.

Late in the afternoon, Philippe "Pipot" Ste. Surin came to see me. His house fell down, but his family is all okay. I gave him my last 2000 HTGs, plus 25 HTGs in change to recharge his phone. I really hope the banks will reopen soon.

I also used someone's Blackberry to access Facebook. It was wonderful to hear from so many sweet friends with messages of faith, encouragement and support. I am truly, truly blessed. Now I must finish prayers and prepare for sleep.

Sunday, 24 January

8 am. I am waiting for Raphael at Ste. Trinite. I looked into the cathedral, but the entire roof has come down, and it doesn't look like it will be possible to salvage the prior bishops' relics for the bishop, at least not yet. I will try to look again, later, from the back of the ruins.

Rico called and said he has to work at the palace today and cannot help me go to look at my apartment, which is just as well.

When Raphael gets here, I will first look for my meds, then climb to the second floor and look at the entrance to EMST to see what it looks like and if our ideas are feasible.

I am sitting with Stevens, a Petit Chanteurs alto, who has lost his entire family to the earthquake.

A little later: Okay. I went into the Ecôle de Musique Ste. Trinite. I found some cases, some music, and a clarinet in the new practice room section.

Then I tried to cross into the older section, but it is now totally blocked.

Then Delinois brought me over to the *Rue des Miracles* (street of miracles) side of the school and showed me that the Salle Ste. Cecile was almost ground level now and had an opening through which you could see the piano where I had been sitting just before the quake (which is now against the back wall).

This hit me hard, and both tears and shivers attacked me. Sometimes reality bites hard!

I still could not find my meds, so I will have only five more weeks here, unless I can manage to find some more when a pharmacy reopens.

I did find some olives, some honey, some toilet paper, some salsa, some plastic cups and bags. I gave them all to the Eveque.

4 pm Mass at College St. Pierre. So sweet to receive my Lord!

I began a Petit Ecôle today at College Ste. Pierre, teaching the children some simple solfege and songs. We will continue every afternoon with this.

Adventure Continues

8:15 am Monday, 25 January, I arrived at Ste. Trinite, sat down and said my daily Rosary. David and Pipot have not yet arrived, so at 9 am I went to *Rue des Miracles* to attempt re-entry into the Music School.

Several people tried to stop me, but then a young man with one leg, Jhonny, hopped up and helped me tremendously. I must see to his future success in every way possible.

We rescued some percussion equipment (not the timpani, though, because they are really stuck in the rubble at the back of stage right!), some trumpet and sax cases (but looters had stolen the instruments, sadly), mutes, mouthpieces and two basses.

These are the two basses that were being used by my godson Remy Jean and his bass teacher, Ariane Saul, when the quake arrived.

One is still playable; the other needs repairs, but will be playable again, too.

Delinois helped bring some back to EST, the rest are in the garage across the the Professional School for now.

I'm exhausted and thirsty and hungry. Pere David just arrived and I told him we can still rescue the stage lighting if we can get wrenches. (They fell, but hit nothing and so are not broken).

So, perhaps, one more trip inside. God give me the strength!

The smell of death has faded to a strong smell like beef jerky. Of course, all the dead have been baking under the sun for two weeks now.

I then saw a very disturbing sight: an animal had chewed on what appeared to be a human arm bone (most of the flesh had been stripped away).

Once again, though, I found no sign of my student, Dominique's body. If it is there, it is buried too deep under the rubble to be seen for now.

Now I am waiting for Florence (who is returning my rent money) and Pappy Gerard (to see if the gift shop is intact enough to use for a storage area). Once that happens, maybe I can go back to College Ste. Pierre and get cleaned up and change.

Oh, one funny note: I ripped the back of my trousers getting out of the school (and my underwear and a bit of my skin, too) on a projecting metal re-bar. We all had a good laugh about how "Now I am a REAL Haitian!"

Pappy Gerard came, but he doesn't have the key to the gift shop. Then Pere David came and after he heard and saw what I had done getting instruments out of the music school, he rallied a dozen or so young men to join the effort.

They even found another, easier way to get into the school, by the toilets, although all the instruments were still passed out through the opening by the rear of the stage, the same way I had brought them out with Jhonny, the one-legged young man.

Meanwhile, Remy Jean, my godson, brought me 4 bags of water, a *Malta* (a canned, non-alcoholic malt beverage) and an egg sandwich. I drank two waters plus the Malta and ate the egg sandwich (which tasted great), then passed the other two waters to Jhonny.

We got many, many more instruments out: even parts from the repair shop and much music, too. Even the photos of Hughes Leroy and Sister Anne Marie were salvaged.

I took a flute (one of the few instruments that had survived in playable condition) that had been brought out, put it together, and played "Amazing Grace" right on the Rue des Miracles, declaring "Now the music will never stop again!"

After several hours of our working in the music school, a large truck arrived to collect salvaged desks and chairs from the professional school, and most of the men who were helping us went there to help.

We will finish, or at least do more, tomorrow (Tuesday).

Remy walked me about half-way back to College Ste. Pierre, and then Carl-Henri met us and brought me home to the college, although we had to detour through a warren of passageways, since the back entrance to the college had been blocked off.

Along the way, we saw a huge U.N. food distribution point (for 50 lb bags of rice). Tens of thousands of people were waiting in line for their turn to receive this precious commodity.

We arrived back at the college cafeteria (bishop's office now, but the staff eats there) at about 3 pm. I drank at least 6 glasses of juice (lime mixed with grapefruit, I think), ate 2 meatballs, a little lettuce and some rice and beans.

Then, with the help of one of the ladies who worked for the seminary, I took a shower and changed, after which I returned to my tent and fell fast asleep.

Two hours later, Carl-Henri woke me to say that Flo had come and gone, but would come back Tuesday morning. I had some very weird dreams that night.

In my dreams I am back in the Ecôle de Musique, in the Salle Ste. Cecile. There is the thick, choking dust that was there after the quake. People are searching through the rubble, looking for...what?

Then they come upon my dead body and I realize that everything I've done in the past weeks has been done only by my spirit, and that I, in fact, am dead and have been so ever since the first quake.

It's a very odd feeling, and perhaps something of survivor's guilt, I guess, but haunting none the less.

I woke in the night to a mild tremor and my ears popped. I

hope it's just congestion from all the dust in the school and not a sign of another quake: everyone is talking about how CNN has predicted there is an 80% chance of another quake hitting us. I hope they are wrong!

Tuesday, 25 January

Today I should be able to pick up my replacement SIM for my cell phone and get my original number back. I got up before 6 am, and went to use the toilet, but the building is locked, so I came back to write in my journal instead.

I will try again soon.

I spoke at length with the Bishop about my calling and how I can best serve God's Will and Haiti. He will pray for me and we will discuss this again.

I walked to Ste. Trinite via the Champs des Mars, and past the Petit Seminaire (which is also ruined).

Salvage work continues at the Professional School and at the music school.

They are bringing out chairs, tables, even some computers now. *Se bon bagay.* ("It's a good thing.")

Soon I will re-enter EMST to search for more instruments, and perhaps find Dominique. There were two tremors this morning. I pray no more come.

I scavenged more instruments from the storage rooms under the back of the auditorium, from the old practice rooms and from

Pierre and Guerlain's office. Then I searched Nicole's office and the treasurer's office, in which I found drumsticks, reeds, and office supplies.

Finally I ventured into Manmi Rose's office. I found a number of Suzuki violins on the left side of the office and brought those out to safety.

I saw one more, smaller size violin on the other side of her desk, near the wall that was by the staircase. I leaned across to grab the case with my left hand, and placed my right hand on the top of the desk to support me....

The desk and the office itself began to tilt down into the ruined stairwell...

Panic!

I grabbed the violin case and backed out the doorway, and realized that this, finally, was enough for me.

Outside, in the street, I met Stephen and Tracey Davenport, who used to volunteer many years ago.

Back at College Ste. Pierre I met Mike Phillips from a company called "Pure Water" which purifies water with an electrolytic process. He was training the boy scouts in the technique, which uses salt and electricity to purify water. It was very interesting.

I also explained to Mike that vaudou is not "devil worship" but a method for honoring ancestors, as exists in many indigenous cultures.

Demolition of EMST

Wednesday, 27 January. We are witnessing the beginning of the demolition of the Ecôle de Musique Sainte Trinite via a huge CAT machine from CNE. Tears.

I saw Shirley (our timpanist in OPST), and Reggie Dulond (who plays tenor sax and repairs instruments) and Shadrac (whose ankle is better!). Hugs and more tears.

We salvaged many of the stage lights.

I paid many of the workers from my pocket:

> Delinois, Jhonny, Carlot each 1000 HTGS (about
> $25 US)
> 300 HTGs to each worker and 400HTGs to the
> man who served as a foreman.

I also gave $100 US cash to Pipot so he can attend truck driver school. (All this was out of the rent money which Florence returned to me)

Miraculously the workers had found my calendar book (With all the papers and photos intact inside!)

Dare I hope that they will also find my Zn5 cell phone? Probably not, but God's Will be done.

I also met a beautiful American photo-journalist named Alison Wright who took my picture in front of the ruined piano and asked about the school. (She reminded me a great deal of my friend, Bonnie Lowell, who is on the board of directors for ICInc). She works as a freelancer for many magazines, including the Smithsonian Magazine and National Geographic.

Thursday, 28 January

I met Remy Jean, my godson, at Ste. Trinite and we took a *tap-tap* up to Petion Ville to purchase supplies for the little school at College Ste. Pierre. Vanessa at Stecher Company on *Rue Lamarre* helped me choose construction paper, copy paper, pens and pencils, colored pencils and crayons, scissors and rulers and protractors and tape and stickers and lollipops(for post-class treats).

I found the photography studio of Philippe Elie (Florence's brother) and had a beer with him, then had dinner with Remy at the Fin Gourmet restaurant, owned by the lovely and gracious Miriam Basile .

Then we rode the *tap-tap* back down to the Ville, to *Rue Lalue* and walked back to the College Ste. Pierre.

Friday, 29 January

I was hoping to go to Jacmel with Gaguy this weekend, but Pere David said we will play a concert at Bel Air, so I have been trying to get a ride to Thomassin to pick up my trumpet. If all else fails Florence will bring it tomorrow morning for me.

This morning, at 10 am, we began regular classes with the Petit Ecôle at the College Ste Pierre. We made the covers for each child's personal book , titled "Mon Livre." They each chose their favorite color of paper, then decorated the covers with pictures and stickers. Tomorrow we will begin to write and draw for the insides of the books. I hope these books will be somewhat thera-peutic as I ask the children to tell the stories of their experiences during the tremblement.

We also reviewed the Danish Alleluia, Joyful Joyful We Adore Thee, and Mon Ami Pierrot.

Strangely, for the first time in a while I am feeling really hungry to-day. Perhaps it is because I ate a real, complete meal yesterday for the first time in weeks. I am waiting for Janet to serve the meal. She served "la bouïlle" (porridge) for breakfast, but I kept my resolve and didn't take anything but water for breakfast. I remain determined to eat only once per day. People are remarking on the physical and spiritual changes in me.

Although I must confess that yesterday at Ste. Trinite I lost my temper at an old "*dlo-boy*" (person selling water packets) who wouldn't stop screaming, even when asked politely to do so. God forgive me, I even used some bad language with him (but everyone laughed, so it helped to break some of the tension).

Every evening, around 6:30 or 7 pm, various people in different parts of the camp begin to sing hymns. It's especially moving for me to hear them sing the "Hatikvah" with Kreyol lyrics and "Alleluia" on the choruses.

Last night, around 8:30 pm, the Boy Scout troop began singing in 4-part a-capella on hymns in Spanish, French and Kreyol. It was so beautiful that I didn't mind the fact that it woke me from a sound sleep!

Friday, 29 January, Evening

Today I spoke with Monseigneur. He told me that his wife's leg is much worse. They have moved her to the the USN Hospital ship "Comfort" in the port. I prayed for her, with him as proxy, and will begin a Novena for her sake today.

Her leg was crushed and stripped (the "stocking injury") so it is worrisome to say the least! But I believe in miracles, and have seen so many of them these past 2 ½ weeks. I know she will be healed, though she may not be whole (crushed limbs, particularly when degloved, often must be amputated).

But I will ask the Blessed Mother to intercede with our Heavenly Father to make her both well and whole, in Jesus' Holy Name. Amen.

Saturday, 30 January

I keep thinking of Jhonny, hopping nimbly up and down the ruins on his one leg, his crutch perched precariously on the edge of an unstable stack, like a mountain goat, sure of his footing even when the ground beneath him is crumbling.

Hunger stalks me, tempting me to give in, but I am holding. The hunger is so real, though, that it is almost a separate entity from me, with its own personality: "Eat!"

"So, I'm supposed to sit here and watch you waste away?" Like a good Jewish or Italian Mama "Djeet?" (Did you eat?).

But somehow I visualize him as a big, jolly man, with a big belly and a bigger laugh. I call him "Harold" (not really, but it's kind of funny to think of "Harold Hunger" and laughter is good). Anyway, he's being a pest right now and I really wish he'd leave me alone.

Sometimes, I've found, going for long, long walks (for 2 hours or more) and praying makes the hunger go away for a few more hours beyond the walk. I do get very thirsty and make sure that I drink a lot of water, so that I don't become dehydrated. The water also helps with the hunger pangs, since filling the belly with water mimics the feeling of food for a while.

I went to Petion Ville via taxi, traveling through Delmas which looks like it's been hit by bombs. Terrible, terrible destruction one block, then nothing at all the next. One house is crumbled to dust, the next is fine. There seems to be neither rhyme nor reason to the destruction at all.

David Saintilus assisted me as we purchased more school supplies, had lunch at Fin Gourmet again, and then we rode the tap-tap back into town.

Sunday, 31 January

Mass this morning happened behind the ruins of the Sainte Trinite Cathedral, and was so poignant. Afterwards I had lunch with Pere David and Thara and Williams at Olaffson's Restaurant. While we were there, eating, we met a Canadian photojournalist named Natasha who was very interested to hear about Ste. Trinite.

When I came back to College Ste. Pierre again, I met Janice Carson, a nurse from Kansas City, Missouri, and we talked for a very long time about my experiences and my patients' injuries.

Then I met the famous journalist Don Wood, from NBC News (interesting to see someone I had seen on TV so many times, reporting from the front lines all over the world!), who was doing a story about the new water systems at the college.

He said he would visit our Petit Ecôle the next day (but he never came).

I also talked with Dr. Fred Sorrells at the Cathedral today. He has worked for a number of years at Ste. Vincent's Home for the Handicapped, and will be working with us on the new school in Jacmel the Caribbean University for the Arts at Jacmel Haiti (CUAJH), which will now include a Sports Complex and Rehabilitation Center. When I told Gaguy Depestre and Fritz Valescot about this, they became very excited.

I enjoyed great theological discussions with both David and Fred today. God is great and continues to move here in Haïti.

I must finish saying my Rosary and then go to sleep.

New Routine

On Monday morning, the first of February, I was amazed to find that we had over 100 children report for the Petit Ecôle. Tuesday, I had Marie and Mackendie (Seminary students) run the school for the day, since I had to attend a staff meeting at Ste. James for all of the Ste. Trinite Music School staff. It was a blessing to see Jean Bernard, Esther, Jerilyn, Ariane, Mr. Dubois, Myriam and all!

On Wednesday, we had a brass ensemble rehearsal at Ste. James. I played Pipot Ste. Surin's trumpet, which was a really bad instrument, in serious need of a valve alignment. It will be great when we have the new school up and running and we will be able to make repairs on instruments like this.

Press Interviews

Today, Tuesday, February 2nd, I passed out some early balloons in the school, which we will use to talk about wind instruments as well as the mini-concert today at 1 pm with the brass ensemble.

Yesterday I saw Phil Elie again in Petion Ville. He said he will try to come to the concert in Bel Air tomorrow and take some photos for us to put up on FaceBook.

He really is a very sweet and good person, and I truly feel he is my little brother, as Florence has become a big sister to me.

I am hopeful that Gaguy will be able to come to the concert this afternoon, too. Florence has said that she is coming.

Lalanne helped me translate the regulations for the Petit Ecôle into French so that we can read them to the children today. They are basically restatements of the golden rule, of course, but also address raising hands to answer questions, not grabbing for the snacks at the end of the day, and setting a good example for others.

At 4:30 pm I received a call from Dr. Fred Sorrells. He said he will come by this evening with another friend to talk about the plans for the new university in Jacmel (CUAJH), the Sports Complex and Para-Olympics.

I also received a phone call this morning from a reporter with the Willimantic Chronicle newspaper, requesting an interview. I apologized, and explained that I was in school, but I would be happy to speak with him if he called back between 5 and 7 pm this evening.

I was also interviewed today by Mandalit Del Barco, from NPR. This interview will air on Saturday morning.

She will bring letters from some children in California for my students. We will ask the older students to respond with letters of their own. She also plans to cover the concert in Bel-Air tomorrow.

The children in the school adored the balloons today. I will try to have balloons once per week, probably on Jeudi (Thursday), so we will call Jeudi "joue day" (pun intended).

At 5 pm, I met Mariano Vales, an orchestra conductor from OAS (Organization of American States). He is a very handsome and charming young man from Argentina's renowned orchestral training program. OAS is sponsoring the concert tomorrow.

I was very amused when he asked me if I was the "Famous Jeanne" whose family is "all-over FaceBook."

Ariane and I spoke a bit about post traumatic stress syndrome. She said she is doing better, but still has some shaky moments. I told her I was the same.

She said she dreams that everything is as it was before the earthquake. I said that is normal, since the change was so sudden and so profound that there was no time to process it all.

I held and hugged her for a while as she sat on my lap like a small child.

Fred arrived at 7 pm, just as I was giving an interview to "Dave" from the Willimantic Chronicle. When I was finished with the interview, he introduced me to a Haïtian man who has written a song which he wants me to orchestrate for the Para-Olympics for next year's games.

Fred has a donor in the US who will help build CUAJH if we include a Sports Complex and Rehabilitation Center. Fritz Valescot has confirmed that there is sufficient land available to do so. Perhaps it might also be possible to locate a campus of Quisqueya University in Jacmel, too. I will address this with Laënnec when he returns from Paris.

Closure and Souvenir

So many, many times I returned to the ruins of the Ste Trinite Complex. Always I was drawn to the same spot: between what had been the right hand side of the auditorium and the business/computer school classrooms.

The laborers who struggled to salvage wires, re-bar and whatever else could be gleaned from the rubble grew accustomed to seeing me come to the site, searching to see if I could find any sign of my lost student.

On Friday, the 29th of March, the large "Cat" backhoe unearthed the second floor down from the collapsed roof of the computer/business school, which connected to the hallway from the right side of the Salle Ste Cecile auditorium from which my student had fled during the earthquake.

As I watched from a bit of a distance, one of the ground laborers shouted and pointed, stopping the CAT operator.

The backhoe had revealed a body: the shattered remains of my student, Dominique Lexide.

Dominique was in several pieces: his skull was separated from his neck, his left arm was missing, his legs were separated from his trunk.

But there was no mistaking the clothing he had been wearing during jazz band rehearsal. At long last I had found my missing student.

Tears, and prayers of committal before his remains, too, were added to the mass grave on the grounds of the school.

I wept all that night for the lost potential of this remarkable young man.

The next night, as I was returning to my sleeping area after another tremor (this one was about a magnitude 3.0), I tripped over something and fell and broke the radius bone of my left arm.

I landed with my palm upward, so that the force of the fall was directly onto the base of my palm. I heard a loud "crack" and the pain was instantaneous and severe.

"OW, oh my sweet Jesus—oh, Lord, it hurts!"

The caretaker, Josue, came running as did the night guard.

They tried to help me get up, but the pain was too severe to move at first.

Then Josue called Dickins Princivil, my Haitian composer friend. I had conducted the premier performance of the orchestral version of his piece "Transitions" on a memorial concert in November of 2009.

Dickins came over and because the hospital would not be open until morning, brought anesthetic ointment and an Ace bandage to help stabilize my arm.

That night Dickins sat vigil all night with me as I tried to sleep.

In the morning we went to the General Hospital, to obtain an x-ray and see one of the American doctors in the emergency room.

It hurt to move-it hurt to sit. I could not find a comfortable position, and the queue of people waiting for the next available doctor was long and moved from seat to seat as people were called.

I leaned against a wall and tried to stay calm and still with breathing exercises.

Finally a young nurse came to talk to me.

"What seems to be the problem?"

A translator started to speak to me in Kreyol, but I told them that I spoke English.

"I think I broke my wrist"

"Yup. It certainly looks that way. I broke my wrist and it really hurts a lot, doesn't it? You'll be okay, though: they'll x-ray to be sure, and then reduce the fracture and cast it."

Sure enough, the x-ray showed a clean break: I had snapped the end of the radius bone right off.

The ER doctor put a temporary cast on my arm and told me to come back to the hospital in the morning to see an orthopedist at the orthopedic clinic, which was only open Monday through Friday.

While the doctor was casting my arm, Pere David Cesar arrived to offer his support. He suggested taking me to the home of Gladys Lauture, and called her to make arrangements.

While he was talking to Gladys, she suggested calling a friend of hers, Dr. Lalane, who was a retired orthopedic surgeon who could come over, look at the x-ray and examine my arm.

This was arranged for that very morning.

The ER nurse fashioned a sort of sling for my arm out of a disposable robe and we left for Gladys' house.

When we arrived, the Dr. Lalane, the doctor was waiting for us.

He looked at my arm, then the x-ray, then again at my arm.

"Your arm is broken: you have broken the end of the radius bone. Your arm must be reduced by an orthopedist, and then cast."

"Reduced? What does that mean?"

He explained that the doctor would have to apply local anesthetic, then traction, then push the bone back together.

I cringed.

Gladys suggested I might like to return to the US for a surgical consultation.

"You could fly out, have your arm fixed and come back, all

within a few days."

I cringed again.

"Go on an airplane? With this? It hurts just to walk or ride in a car. How am I going to tolerate an airplane ride?"

Then the retired doctor offered an alternative.

"Well, there is 'Velo'…"

"Velo?"

"Dr. Jean Philippe Harvel "Velo" Duverseau an orthopedic surgeon in Petion Ville."

Gladys went to her office to make the call.

And so I met Dr. "Velo" Duverseau, a wonderful young orthopedic surgeon who had been busy with amputations of infected limbs of earthquake victims.

Velo is a striking man, tall and sturdily built, with dark hair with a couple of streaks of white.

He is gracious and his manner immediately set me at ease, even as he explained the process of correcting my injury. He warned me that it would hurt when he had to inject the novacaine into my wrist (local anesthetic).

My friend and colleague, Janet Anthony, who had first invited me to Haiti, was visiting for a week during her spring vacation and offered me her strong left hand to squeeze as the anesthetic was injected and until it took effect.

Velo instructed Janet to pull on my fingers as she pushed against my upper arm (to produce traction). He then applied firm, steady pressure from my hand toward the lower arm to align the bones.

Remarkably, even though I could not feel anything at that particular site, my entire body relaxed once the pieces of bone were realigned again.

Velo then applied antiseptic to the arm, a band-aid over the injection site, and cast my arm into what he described as a "neutral" position.

He handed me some painkillers, and told me to rest for the rest of the day, but to return to the hospital Monday morning for another x-ray to test the alignment.

Once we had the x-ray, we were to return to his office so he could check the alignment.

Of course, the x-ray showed that the alignment was perfect: he had done a great job!

Velo had me return weekly to check on my progress, each time having me use my fingers a bit more.

On April 14th, he removed the original cast, checked my arm for progress, and put on a new cast for my trip back to the United States on April 16th.

We parted with a hug and a promise that when I returned to Haiti I would spend an evening with him to play trumpet while he played piano.

I have thought a lot about why I fell and broke my arm at this point when I had been in precarious positions so many times over the months since the earthquake, and indeed had been in great danger during the earthquake itself.

Somehow I feel that the physical pain of having a broken arm was easier to handle than the emotional pain of the guilt of having shouted "Run" to my students when the earthquake happened.

The only student who ran was Dominique, and thus I had spent months feeling that it was my fault he died.

Perhaps, I reasoned, if I had not shouted "Run" he would have crouched down, in place, as did the other students and he would still be alive today.

Perhaps not. Pastor Harold told me back in January: "It is not your will, but God's Will that was done."

In any event, my injuries are healing, as are Haiti's. It takes time and care and effort, but I truly believe that all will be as it should be.

Afterword

Three Months Later

Now that we are in April, we are settling into a bit more of a routine of life: life that is changed, there can be no question, but it is life none the less.

Food is somewhat more available, thanks to NGO's, UNICEF, UN and UNESCO. Clean water is also available in many places, thanks to the efforts of World Vision, people like Mike Phillips with his water treatment methods (Hays Pure Water for All) and the large tank-treatment programs of Water Missions International.

We still shudder and avert our eyes from collapsed buildings, for the horror continues to assault us on every side.

Yet, somehow the sites which have been completely demolished can be even more painful evidence of loss: in the flatness of rubble strewn with pieces of bones, occasionally bits of dried flesh and here and there a human skull is revealed.

And the demolition of ruined buildings continues, 24/7. Sometimes you wake in the night, wondering if you are experiencing another "tremblement" only to realize that it is the sound of machines felling buildings, rather than the earth itself, and settle back down to more uneasy rest.

Sometimes, of course, there are actual tremors that wake you in the middle of the night or in the early morning. Your body responds before your mind can grasp what is happening: your heart races, your breath quickens, your body starts and moves toward the doorway at the speed of instinct.

There are, of course, still places where the smell of death is apparent: collapsed houses where the moisture continues to support the ongoing corruption of those lost within.

And when buildings are demolished that contain cadavers, as those cadavers are exposed, so is the scent of their demise. We have all become too well-acquainted with that smell, having breathed it on a daily basis for so long.

Sadly, there is scarcely a single fallen building that does not contain some bodies, which is another reason why those of us who have worked in the Ville are so convinced that the death toll is far, far higher than the government will admit (probably more like 1,300,000 than the 300,000 admitted to by the government).

There are also greater numbers of homeless, literally, than ever before. Shacks of scrap wood, scrap tin, bed sheets, and (for those lucky enough to have found one) a plastic tarp abound all throughout the capital area (which includes Port-au-Prince itself and all the metropolitan neighborhoods, Delmas, Bourdon, Petion Ville, Cite Soleil, Bel-Air, Frere, Martissant, Carrefour, etc.)

More children beg in the streets, even more pitifully, since many of them are new to the game, not the seasoned veterans of long-term begging and prostitution who cling to their established territories ferociously.

And sadly, some of the smaller religious sects have taken the tack of "accusatory evangelism." Spouting the fallacious claim that "It is the fault of them not us," with various sects accusing Catholics, or Episcopalians, or Seventh Day Adventists or Voudouissants or whomever of having caused God's wrath via the earthquake to strike down sinners. They are forgetting, of course, that every part of society experienced losses: every denomination faced fallen houses of worship, lost members, and suffered from the earthquake and its aftermath.

Interestingly, it is the Voudouissants who show the greatest tolerance and love toward their fellow beings of any of the religious sects, with the exception of the Episcopalians, who do not judge, but work to serve their fellow beings.

And once, again, I must draw attention to the beloved and saintly leader of the Episcopal Church of Haiti: Bishop Jean Zaché Duracin. This loving, erudite, faithful man, who lived and served his flock from within, continues to inspire us and give us hope on a daily basis. Truly, truly he is a worthy example of Christ's Love among us!

There are pressing crime issues, sadly. Gangs have sprung up again, since many of their previously imprisoned leaders escaped during the earthquake when the prison split open.

Yet all is not lost: more and more Haïtians are taking proactive stances in planning and executing changes for the better in their communities.

The earthquake was a natural phenomenon, not a supernatural one. I have seen so many miracles of every sort over the past three months that I strongly believe God's healing Hand is present here.

But that Hand is not administering punishment, but healing! And God's Word speaks of Love, not retribution! (Ultimately, Christ's sacrifice on the Cross changed everything, for all eternity.)

Those of us who are *"etrangers"* (foreigners), who remained here after the earthquake to help, or arrived after the quake to intervene or offer assistance, are witnesses to God's Almighty Presence here; to the strength, power and resilience of the human spirit; to the power of love in every manifestation.

As my new friend, Dr. Jean Philippe Harvel "Velo" Duverseau says

> "Those of us who survived being in the tremblement have been charged with two duties: the first is, of course, to serve the Lord our God; the second is to serve our fellow beings."

That service continues, and multiplies as each of us shares our witness with the world.

Haïti's travails grant each of us the opportunity to step forward and serve, in whatever way may be possible; to make use of our God-given talents in a way that is beneficial to others, not just to ourselves or our pocketbook; to truly experience the sensation of being God's representatives on earth:

- participating in the process of creation rather than destruction
- of hope rather than despair
- of unity and solidarity rather than divisiveness and antagonism
- of love and encouragement and possibilities to be explored and developed.

I believe that Haïti will rise again, to be a leader in the world for cultural and spiritual and creative and educational endeavors. But this cannot happen if the world turns a blind eye and deaf ear toward her.

We must all join in the advocacy. We must all share the story of brave little Haïti, her triumphs and her trials.

We each have the ability to make a real difference in the world!

Peace, love and blessings, Jeanne

LaVergne, TN USA
07 December 2010
207641LV00003B/21/P